Algorithms Illuminated
Part 2: Graph Algorithms and Data Structures

Tim Roughgarden

First Edition

Cover image: *Untitled*, by Nick Terry

ISBN: 978-0-9992829-2-2 (Paperback)
ISBN: 978-0-9992829-3-9 (ebook)

Library of Congress Control Number: 2017914282

Soundlikeyourself Publishing, LLC
San Francisco, CA
soundlikeyourselfpublishing@gmail.com
www.algorithmsilluminated.org

In memory of James Wesley Shean
(1921–2010)

Contents

Preface

This book is the second of a four-part series based on my online algorithms courses that have been running regularly since 2012, which in turn are based on an undergraduate course that I've taught many times at Stanford University. The first part of the series is not a prerequisite for this one, and this book should be accessible to any reader who has the background described in the "Who Are You?" section below and is familiar with asymptotic notation (which is reviewed in Appendix C).

What We'll Cover

Algorithms Illuminated, Part 2 provides an introduction to and basic literacy in the following three topics.

Graph search and applications. Graphs model many different types of networks, including road networks, communication networks, social networks, and networks of dependencies between tasks. Graphs can get complex, but there are several blazingly fast primitives for reasoning about graph structure. We begin with linear-time algorithms for searching a graph, with applications ranging from network analysis to task sequencing.

Shortest paths. In the shortest-path problem, the goal is to compute the best route in a network from point A to point B. The problem has obvious applications, like computing driving directions, and also shows up in disguise in many more general planning problems. We'll generalize one of our graph search algorithms and arrive at Dijkstra's famous shortest-path algorithm.

Data structures. This book will make you an educated client of several different data structures for maintaining an evolving set of objects with keys. The primary goal is to develop your intuition about which data structure is the right one for your application. The optional advanced sections provide guidance in how to implement these data structures from scratch.

We first discuss heaps, which can quickly identify the stored object with the smallest key and are useful for sorting, implementing a priority queue, and implementing Dijkstra's algorithm in near-linear time. Search trees maintain a total ordering over the keys of the stored objects and support an even richer array of operations. Hash tables are optimized for super-fast lookups and are ubiquitous in modern programs. We'll also cover the bloom filter, a close cousin of the hash table that uses less space at the expense of occasional errors.

For a more detailed look into the book's contents, check out the "Upshot" sections that conclude each chapter and highlight the most important points. The starred sections of the book are the most advanced ones. The time-constrained reader can skip these on a first reading without loss of continuity.

Topics covered in the other three parts. *Algorithms Illuminated, Part 1* covers asymptotic notation (big-O notation and its close cousins), divide-and-conquer algorithms and the master method, randomized QuickSort and its analysis, and linear-time selection algorithms. *Part 3* focuses on greedy algorithms (scheduling, minimum spanning trees, clustering, Huffman codes) and dynamic programming (knapsack, sequence alignment, shortest paths, optimal search trees). *Part 4* is all about NP-completeness, what it means for the algorithm designer, and strategies for coping with computationally intractable problems, including the analysis of heuristics and local search.

Skills You'll Learn

Mastering algorithms takes time and effort. Why bother?

Become a better programmer. You'll learn several blazingly fast subroutines for processing data as well as several useful data structures for organizing data that you can deploy directly in your own programs. Implementing and using these algorithms will stretch and improve your programming skills. You'll also learn general algorithm design paradigms that are relevant for many different problems across different domains, as well as tools for predicting the performance of such algorithms. These "algorithmic design patterns" can help you come up with new algorithms for problems that arise in your own work.

Sharpen your analytical skills.   You'll get lots of practice describing and reasoning about algorithms. Through mathematical analysis, you'll gain a deep understanding of the specific algorithms and data structures covered in these books. You'll acquire facility with several mathematical techniques that are broadly useful for analyzing algorithms.

Think algorithmically.   After you learn about algorithms, it's hard to not see them everywhere, whether you're riding an elevator, watching a flock of birds, managing your investment portfolio, or even watching an infant learn. Algorithmic thinking is increasingly useful and prevalent in disciplines outside of computer science, including biology, statistics, and economics.

Literacy with computer science's greatest hits.   Studying algorithms can feel like watching a highlight reel of many of the greatest hits from the last sixty years of computer science. No longer will you feel excluded at that computer science cocktail party when someone cracks a joke about Dijkstra's algorithm. After reading these books, you'll know exactly what they mean.

Ace your technical interviews.   Over the years, countless students have regaled me with stories about how mastering the concepts in these books enabled them to ace every technical interview question they were ever asked.

How These Books Are Different

This series of books has only one goal: *to teach the basics of algorithms in the most accessible way possible.* Think of them as a transcript of what an expert algorithms tutor would say to you over a series of one-on-one lessons.

There are a number of excellent more traditional and encyclopedic textbooks on algorithms, any of which usefully complement this book series with additional details, problems, and topics. I encourage you to explore and find your own favorites. There are also several books that, unlike these books, cater to programmers looking for ready-made algorithm implementations in a specific programming language. Many such implementations are freely available on the Web as well.

Who Are You?

The whole point of these books and the online courses upon which they are based is to be as widely and easily accessible as possible. People of all ages, backgrounds, and walks of life are well represented in my online courses, and there are large numbers of students (high-school, college, etc.), software engineers (both current and aspiring), scientists, and professionals hailing from all corners of the world.

This book is not an introduction to programming, and ideally you've acquired basic programming skills in a standard language (like Java, Python, C, Scala, Haskell, etc.). For a litmus test, check out Section 8.2—if it makes sense, you'll be fine for the rest of the book. If you need to beef up your programming skills, there are several outstanding free online courses that teach basic programming.

We also use mathematical analysis as needed to understand how and why algorithms really work. The freely available book *Mathematics for Computer Science*, by Eric Lehman, F. Thomson Leighton, and Albert R. Meyer is an excellent and entertaining refresher on mathematical notation (like $\sum$ and $\forall$), the basics of proofs (induction, contradiction, etc.), discrete probability, and much more.

Additional Resources

These books are based on online courses that are currently running on the Coursera and Stanford Lagunita platforms. I've made several resources available to help you replicate as much of the online course experience as you like.

Videos. If you're more in the mood to watch and listen than to read, check out the YouTube video playlists available from www.algorithmsilluminated.org. These videos cover all of the topics of this book series, as well as additional advanced topics. I hope they exude a contagious enthusiasm for algorithms that, alas, is impossible to replicate fully on the printed page.

Quizzes. How can you know if you're truly absorbing the concepts in this book? Quizzes with solutions and explanations are scattered throughout the text; when you encounter one, I encourage you to pause and think about the answer before reading on.

End-of-chapter problems. At the end of each chapter you'll find several relatively straightforward questions for testing your understanding, followed by harder and more open-ended challenge problems. Solutions to problems that are marked with an *"(S)"* appear at the end of the book. Readers can interact with me and each other about the remaining end-of-chapter problems through the book's discussion forum (see below).

Programming problems. Most of the chapters conclude with a suggested programming project, whose goal is to help you develop a detailed understanding of an algorithm by creating your own working implementation of it. Data sets, along with test cases and their solutions, can be found at www.algorithmsilluminated.org.

Discussion forums. A big reason for the success of online courses is the opportunities they provide for participants to help each other understand the course material and debug programs through discussion forums. Readers of these books have the same opportunity, via the forums available at www.algorithmsilluminated.org.

Acknowledgments

These books would not exist without the passion and hunger supplied by the hundreds of thousands of participants in my algorithms courses over the years, both on campus at Stanford and on online platforms. I am particularly grateful to those who supplied detailed feedback on an earlier draft of this book: Tonya Blust, Yuan Cao, Jim Humelsine, Vladimir Kokshenev, Bayram Kuliyev, Patrick Monkelban, and Daniel Zingaro.

I always appreciate suggestions and corrections from readers. These are best communicated through the discussion forums mentioned above.

Tim Roughgarden
London, United Kingdom
July 2018

Chapter 7

Graphs: The Basics

This short chapter explains what graphs are, what they are good for, and the most common ways to represent them in a computer program. The next two chapters cover a number of famous and useful algorithms for reasoning about graphs.

7.1 Some Vocabulary

When you hear the word "graph," you probably think about an x-axis, a y-axis, and so on (Figure 7.1(a)). To an algorithms person, a *graph* can also mean a representation of the relationships between pairs of objects (Figure 7.1(b)).

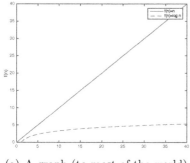

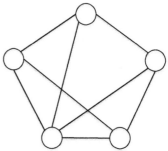

(a) A graph (to most of the world) (b) A graph (in algorithms)

Figure 7.1: In algorithms, a graph is a representation of a set of objects (such as people) and the pairwise relationships between them (such as friendships).

The second type of graph has two ingredients—the objects being represented, and their pairwise relationships. The former are called the *vertices* (singular: vertex) or the *nodes* of the graph.[1] The pairwise relationships translate to the *edges* of the graph. We usually denote the vertex and edge sets of a graph by V and E, respectively, and sometimes write $G = (V, E)$ to mean the graph G with vertices V and edges E.

There are two flavors of graphs, directed and undirected. Both types are important and ubiquitous in applications, so you should know about both of them. In an *undirected* graph, each edge corresponds to an unordered pair $\{v, w\}$ of vertices, which are called the *endpoints* of the edge (Figure 7.2(a)). In an undirected graph, there is no difference between an edge (v, w) and an edge (w, v). In a *directed* graph, each edge (v, w) is an ordered pair, with the edge traveling from the first vertex v (called the *tail*) to the second w (the *head*); see Figure 7.2(b).[2]

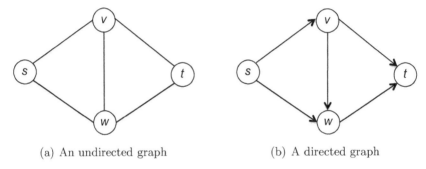

(a) An undirected graph   (b) A directed graph

Figure 7.2: Graphs with four vertices and five edges. The edges of undirected and directed graphs are unordered and ordered vertex pairs, respectively.

7.2   A Few Applications

Graphs are a fundamental concept, and they show up all the time in computer science, biology, sociology, economics, and so on. Here are a few of the countless examples.

---

[1]Having two names for the same thing can be annoying, but both terms are in widespread use and you should be familiar with them. For the most part, we'll stick with "vertices" throughout this book series.

[2]Directed edges are sometimes called *arcs*, but we won't use this terminology in this book series.

Road networks.   When your smartphone's software computes driving directions, it searches through a graph that represents the road network, with vertices corresponding to intersections and edges corresponding to individual road segments.

The World Wide Web.   The Web can be modeled as a directed graph, with the vertices corresponding to individual Web pages, and the edges corresponding to hyperlinks, directed from the page containing the hyperlink to the destination page.

Social networks.   A social network can be represented as a graph whose vertices correspond to individuals and edges to some type of relationship. For example, an edge could indicate a friendship between its endpoints, or that one of its endpoints is a follower of the other. Among the currently popular social networks, which ones are most naturally modeled as an undirected graph, and which ones as a directed graph? (There are interesting examples of both.)

Precedence constraints.   Graphs are also useful in problems that lack an obvious network structure. For example, imagine that you have to complete a bunch of tasks, subject to precedence constraints—perhaps you're a first-year university student, planning which courses to take and in which order. One way to tackle this problem is to apply the topological sorting algorithm described in Section 8.5 to the following directed graph: there is one vertex for each course that your major requires, with an edge directed from course A to course B whenever A is a prerequisite for B.

7.3   Measuring the Size of a Graph

In this book, like in *Part 1*, we'll analyze the running time of different algorithms as a function of the input size. When the input is a single array, as for a sorting algorithm, there is an obvious way to define the "input size," as the array's length. When the input involves a graph, we must specify exactly how the graph is represented and what we mean by its "size."

7.3.1   The Number of Edges in a Graph

Two parameters control a graph's size—the number of vertices and the number of edges. Here is the most common notation for these quantities.

Notation for Graphs

For a graph $G = (V, E)$ with vertex set V and edge set E:

- $n = |V|$ denotes the number of vertices.

- $m = |E|$ denotes the number of edges.[3]

The next quiz asks you to think about how the number m of edges in an undirected graph can depend on the number n of vertices. For this question, we'll assume that there's at most one undirected edge between each pair of vertices—no "parallel edges" are allowed. We'll also assume that the graph is "connected." We'll define this concept formally in Section 8.3; intuitively, it means that the graph is "in one piece," with no way to break it into two parts without any edges crossing between the parts. The graphs in Figures 7.1(b) and 7.2(a) are connected, while the graph in Figure 7.3 is not.

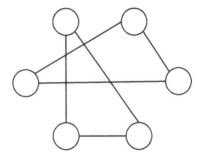

Figure 7.3: An undirected graph that is not connected.

Quiz 7.1

Consider an undirected graph with n vertices and no parallel edges. Assume that the graph is connected, meaning "in one piece." What are the minimum and maximum numbers of edges, respectively, that the graph could have?

---

[3]For a finite set S, $|S|$ denotes the number of elements in S.

a) $n - 1$ and $\frac{n(n-1)}{2}$

b) $n - 1$ and n^2

c) n and 2^n

d) n and n^n

(See Section 7.3.3 for the solution and discussion.)

7.3.2   Sparse vs. Dense Graphs

Now that Quiz 7.1 has you thinking about how the number of edges of a graph can vary with the number of vertices, we can discuss the distinction between *sparse* and *dense* graphs. The difference is important because some data structures and algorithms are better suited for sparse graphs, and others for dense graphs.

Let's translate the solution to Quiz 7.1 into asymptotic notation.[4] First, if an undirected graph with n vertices is connected, the number of edges m is at least linear in n (that is, $m = \Omega(n)$).[5] Second, if the graph has no parallel edges, then $m = O(n^2)$.[6] We conclude that the number of edges in a connected undirected graph with no parallel edges is somewhere between linear and quadratic in the number of vertices.

Informally, a graph is *sparse* if the number of edges is relatively close to linear in the number of vertices, and *dense* if this number is closer to quadratic in the number of vertices. For example, graphs with n vertices and $O(n \log n)$ edges are usually considered sparse, while those with $\Omega(n^2 / \log n)$ edges are considered dense. "Partially dense" graphs, like those with $\approx n^{3/2}$ edges, may be considered either sparse or dense, depending on the specific application.

7.3.3   Solution to Quiz 7.1

Correct answer: (a). In a connected undirected graph with n vertices and no parallel edges, the number m of edges is at least $n - 1$

---

[4]See Appendix C for a review of big-O, big-Omega, and big-Theta notation.

[5]If the graph need not be connected, there could be as few as zero edges.

[6]If parallel edges are allowed, a graph with at least two vertices can have an arbitrarily large number of edges.

and at most $n(n-1)/2$. To see why the lower bound is correct, consider a graph $G = (V, E)$. As a thought experiment, imagine building up G one edge at a time, starting from the graph with vertices V and no edges. Initially, before any edges are added, each of the n vertices is completely isolated, so the graph trivially has n distinct "pieces." Adding an edge (v, w) has the effect of fusing the piece containing v with the piece containing w (Figure 7.4). Thus, each edge addition decreases the number of pieces by at most 1.[7] To get down to a single piece from n pieces, you need to add at least $n-1$ edges. There are plenty of connected graphs that have n vertices and only $n-1$ edges—these are called *trees* (Figure 7.5).

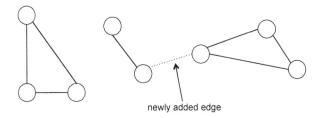

newly added edge

Figure 7.4: Adding a new edge fuses the pieces containing its endpoints into a single piece. In this example, the number of different pieces drops from three to two.

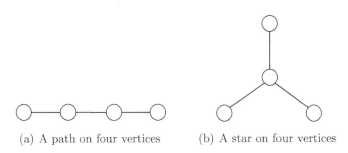

(a) A path on four vertices   (b) A star on four vertices

Figure 7.5: Two connected undirected graphs with four vertices and three edges.

The maximum number of edges in a graph with no parallel edges is achieved by the *complete graph*, with every possible edge present.

---

[7]If both endpoints of the edge are already in the same piece, the number of pieces doesn't decrease at all.

Because there are $\binom{n}{2} = \frac{n(n-1)}{2}$ pairs of vertices in an n-vertex graph, this is also the maximum number of edges. For example, when $n = 4$, the maximum number of edges is $\binom{4}{2} = 6$ (Figure 7.6).[8]

Figure 7.6: The complete graph on four vertices has $\binom{4}{2} = 6$ edges.

7.4   Representing a Graph

There is more than one way to encode a graph for use in an algorithm. In this book series, we'll work primarily with the "adjacency list" representation of a graph (Section 7.4.1), but you should also be aware of the "adjacency matrix" representation (Section 7.4.2).

7.4.1   Adjacency Lists

The *adjacency list* representation of graphs is the dominant one that we'll use in this book series.

Ingredients for Adjacency Lists

1. An array containing the graph's vertices.

2. An array containing the graph's edges.

3. For each edge, a pointer to each of its two endpoints.

4. For each vertex, a pointer to each of the incident edges.

---

[8] $\binom{n}{2}$ is pronounced "n choose 2," and is also sometimes referred to as a "binomial coefficient." To see why the number of ways to choose an unordered pair of distinct objects from a set of n objects is $\frac{n(n-1)}{2}$, think about choosing the first object (from the n options) and then a second, distinct object (from the $n-1$ remaining options). The $n(n-1)$ resulting outcomes produce each pair (x, y) of objects twice (once with x first and y second, once with y first and x second), so there must be $\frac{n(n-1)}{2}$ pairs in all.

The adjacency list representation boils down to two arrays (or linked lists, if you prefer): one for keeping track of the vertices, and one for the edges. These two arrays cross-reference each other in the natural way, with each edge associated with pointers to its endpoints and each vertex with pointers to the edges for which it is an endpoint.

For a directed graph, each edge keeps track of which endpoint is the tail and which endpoint is the head. Each vertex v maintains two arrays of pointers, one for the outgoing edges (for which v is the tail) and one for the incoming edges (for which v is the head).

What are the memory requirements of the adjacency list representation?

Quiz 7.2

How much space does the adjacency list representation of a graph require, as a function of the number n of vertices and the number m of edges?

a) $\Theta(n)$

b) $\Theta(m)$

c) $\Theta(m + n)$

d) $\Theta(n^2)$

(See Section 7.4.4 for the solution and discussion.)

7.4.2 The Adjacency Matrix

Consider an undirected graph $G = (V, E)$ with n vertices and no parallel edges, and label its vertices $1, 2, 3, \ldots, n$. The *adjacency matrix* representation of G is a square $n \times n$ matrix A—equivalently, a two-dimensional array—with only zeroes and ones as entries. Each entry A_{ij} is defined as

$$A_{ij} = \begin{cases} 1 & \text{if edge } (i, j) \text{ belongs to } E \\ 0 & \text{otherwise.} \end{cases}$$

Thus, an adjacency matrix maintains one bit for each pair of vertices, which keeps track of whether or not the edge is present (Figure 7.7).

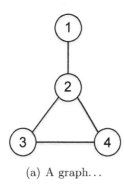

$$\begin{array}{c c c c c}
 & 1 & 2 & 3 & 4 \\
1 & 0 & 1 & 0 & 0 \\
2 & 1 & 0 & 1 & 1 \\
3 & 0 & 1 & 0 & 1 \\
4 & 0 & 1 & 1 & 0
\end{array}$$

(a) A graph...   (b) ...and its adjacency matrix

Figure 7.7: The adjacency matrix of a graph maintains one bit for each vertex pair, indicating whether or not there is an edge connecting the two vertices.

It's easy to add bells and whistles to the adjacency matrix representation of a graph:

- *Parallel edges.* If a graph can have multiple edges with the same pair of endpoints, then A_{ij} can be defined as the number of edges with endpoints i and j.

- *Weighted graphs.* Similarly, if each edge (i, j) has a weight w_{ij}—perhaps representing a cost or a distance—then each entry A_{ij} stores w_{ij}.

- *Directed graphs.* For a directed graph G, each entry A_{ij} of the adjacency matrix is defined as

$$A_{ij} = \begin{cases} 1 & \text{if edge } (i, j) \text{ belongs to } E \\ 0 & \text{otherwise,} \end{cases}$$

where "edge (i, j)" now refers to the edge directed from i to j. Every undirected graph has a symmetric adjacency matrix, while a directed graph usually has an asymmetric adjacency matrix.

What are the memory requirements of an adjacency matrix?

Quiz 7.3

How much space does the adjacency matrix of a graph
require, as a function of the number n of vertices and the
number m of edges?

  a) $\Theta(n)$

  b) $\Theta(m)$

  c) $\Theta(m+n)$

  d) $\Theta(n^2)$

(See Section 7.4.4 for the solution and discussion.)

7.4.3   Comparing the Representations

Confronted with two different ways to represent a graph, you're
probably wondering: Which is better? The answer, as it so often is
with such questions, is "it depends." First, it depends on the density of
your graph—on how the number m of edges compares to the number n
of vertices. The moral of Quizzes 7.2 and 7.3 is that the adjacency
matrix is an efficient way to encode a dense graph but is wasteful for
a sparse graph. Second, it depends on which operations you want to
support. On both counts, adjacency lists make more sense for the
algorithms and applications described in this book series.

Most of our graph algorithms will involve exploring a graph. Adjacency lists are perfect for graph exploration—you arrive at a vertex,
and the adjacency list immediately indicates your options for the next
step.[9] Adjacency matrices do have their applications, but we won't
see them in this book series.[10]

Much of the modern-day interest in fast graph primitives is motivated by massive sparse networks. Consider, for example, the Web
graph (Section 7.2), where vertices correspond to Web pages and
directed edges to hyperlinks. It's hard to get an exact measurement of

---

[9]If you had access to only the adjacency matrix of a graph, how long would it
take you to figure out which edges are incident to a given vertex?

[10]For example, you can count the number of common neighbors of each pair of
vertices in one fell swoop by squaring the graph's adjacency matrix.

the size of this graph, but a conservative lower bound on the number of vertices is 10 billion, or 10^{10}. Storing and reading through an array of this length already requires significant computational resources, but it is well within the limits of what modern computers can do. The size of the adjacency matrix of this graph, however, is proportional to 100 quintillion (10^{20}). This is way too big to store or process with today's technology. But the Web graph is sparse—the average number of outgoing edges from a vertex is well under 100. The memory requirements of the adjacency list representation of the Web graph are therefore proportional to 10^{12} (a trillion). This may be too big for your laptop, but it's within the capabilities of state-of-the-art data-processing systems.[11]

7.4.4   Solutions to Quizzes 7.2–7.3

Solution to Quiz 7.2

Correct answer: (c). The adjacency list representation requires space linear in the size of the graph (meaning the number of vertices plus the number of edges), which is ideal.[12] Seeing this is a little tricky. Let's step through the four ingredients one by one. The vertex and edge arrays have lengths n and m, respectively, and so require $\Theta(n)$ and $\Theta(m)$ space. The third ingredient associates two pointers with each edge (one for each endpoint). These $2m$ pointers contribute an additional $\Theta(m)$ to the space requirement.

The fourth ingredient might make you nervous. After all, each of the n vertices can participate in as many as $n - 1$ edges—one per other vertex—seemingly leading to a bound of $\Theta(n^2)$. This quadratic bound would be accurate in a very dense graph, but is overkill in sparser graphs. The key insight is: *For every vertex→edge pointer in the fourth ingredient, there is a corresponding edge→vertex pointer in the third ingredient.* If the edge e is incident to the vertex v, then e has a pointer to its endpoint v, and, conversely, v has a pointer to the incident edge e. We conclude that the pointers in the third and fourth ingredients are in one-to-one correspondence, and so they require

---

[11]For example, the essence of Google's original **PageRank** algorithm for measuring Web page importance relied on efficient search in the Web graph.

[12]Caveat: The leading constant factor here is larger than that for the adjacency matrix by an order of magnitude.

exactly the same amount of space, namely $\Theta(m)$. The final scorecard is:

vertex array	$\Theta(n)$
edge array	$\Theta(m)$
pointers from edges to endpoints	$\Theta(m)$
+ pointers from vertices to incident edges	$\Theta(m)$
total	$\Theta(m+n)$.

The bound of $\Theta(m+n)$ applies whether or not the graph is connected, and whether or not it has parallel edges.[13]

Solution to Quiz 7.3

Correct answer: (d). The straightforward way to store an adjacency matrix is as an $n \times n$ two-dimensional array of bits. This uses $\Theta(n^2)$ space, albeit with a small hidden constant. For a dense graph, in which the number of edges is itself close to quadratic in n, the adjacency matrix requires space close to linear in the size of the graph. For sparse graphs, however, in which the number of edges is closer to linear in n, the adjacency matrix representation is highly wasteful.[14]

The Upshot

☆ A graph is a representation of the pairwise relationships between objects, such as friendships in a social network, hyperlinks between Web pages, or dependencies between tasks.

☆ A graph comprises a set of vertices and a set of edges. Edges are unordered in undirected graphs and ordered in directed graphs.

☆ A graph is sparse if the number of edges m is close to linear in the number of vertices n, and dense if m is close to quadratic in n.

---

[13]If the graph is connected, then $m \geq n - 1$ (by Quiz 7.1), and we could write $\Theta(m)$ in place of $\Theta(m + n)$.

[14]This waste can be reduced by using tricks for storing and manipulating sparse matrices, meaning matrices with lots of zeroes. For instance, Matlab and Python's SciPy package both support sparse matrix representations.

☆ The adjacency list representation of a graph maintains vertex and edge arrays, cross-referencing each other in the natural way, and requires space linear in the total number of vertices and edges.

☆ The adjacency matrix representation of a graph maintains one bit per pair of vertices to keep track of which edges are present, and requires space quadratic in the number of vertices.

☆ The adjacency list representation is the preferred one for sparse graphs, and for applications that involve graph exploration.

Test Your Understanding

Problem 7.1 *(S)* Let $G = (V, E)$ be an undirected graph. By the *degree* of a vertex $v \in V$, we mean the number of edges in E that are incident to v (i.e., that have v as an endpoint).[15] For each of the following conditions on the graph G, is the condition satisfied only by dense graphs, only by sparse graphs, or by both some sparse and some dense graphs? As usual, $n = |V|$ denotes the number of vertices. Assume that n is large (say, at least 10,000).

a) At least one vertex of G has degree at most 10.

b) Every vertex of G has degree at most 10.

c) At least one vertex of G has degree $n - 1$.

d) Every vertex of G has degree $n - 1$.

Problem 7.2 *(S)* Consider an undirected graph $G = (V, E)$ that is represented as an adjacency matrix. Given a vertex $v \in V$, how many operations are required to identify the edges incident to v? (Let k denote the number of such edges. As usual, n and m denote the number of vertices and edges, respectively.)

---

[15]The abbreviation "i.e." stands for *id est*, and means "that is."

a) $\Theta(1)$

b) $\Theta(k)$

c) $\Theta(n)$

d) $\Theta(m)$

Problem 7.3 Consider a directed graph $G = (V, E)$ represented with adjacency lists, with each vertex storing an array of its outgoing edges (but *not* its incoming edges). Given a vertex $v \in V$, how many operations are required to identify the incoming edges of v? (Let k denote the number of such edges. As usual, n and m denote the number of vertices and edges, respectively).

a) $\Theta(1)$

b) $\Theta(k)$

c) $\Theta(n)$

d) $\Theta(m)$

Chapter 8

Graph Search and Its Applications

This chapter is all about fundamental primitives for graph search and their applications. One very cool aspect of this material is that all the algorithms that we'll cover are blazingly fast (linear time with small constants), and it can be quite tricky to understand why they work! The culmination of this chapter—computing the strongly connected components of a directed graph with only two passes of depth-first search (Section 8.6)—vividly illustrates how fast algorithms often require deep insight into the problem structure.

We begin with an overview section (Section 8.1), which covers some reasons why you should care about graph search, a general strategy for searching a graph without doing any redundant work, and a high-level introduction to the two most important search strategies, breadth-first search (BFS) and depth-first search (DFS). Sections 8.2 and 8.3 describe BFS in more detail, including applications to computing shortest paths and the connected components of an undirected graph. Sections 8.4 and 8.5 drill down on DFS and how to use it to compute a topological ordering of a directed acyclic graph (equivalently, to sequence tasks while respecting precedence constraints). Section 8.6 uses DFS to compute the strongly connected components of a directed graph in linear time. Section 8.7 explains how this fast graph primitive can be used to explore the structure of the Web.

8.1 Overview

This section provides a bird's-eye view of algorithms for graph search and their applications.

8.1.1 Some Applications

Why would we want to search a graph, or to figure out if a graph contains a path from point A to point B? Here are a few of the many,

many reasons.

Checking connectivity. In a physical network, such as a road network or a network of computers, an important sanity check is that you can get anywhere from anywhere else. That is, for every choice of a point A and a point B, there should be a path in the network from the former to the latter.

Connectivity can also be important in abstract (non-physical) graphs that represent pairwise relationships between objects. One network that's fun to play with is the movie network, where vertices correspond to movie actors, and two actors are connected by an undirected edge whenever they appeared in the same movie.[1] For example, how many "degrees of separation" are there between different actors? The most famous statistic of this type is the *Bacon number*, which is the minimum number of hops through the movie network needed to reach the fairly ubiquitous actor Kevin Bacon.[2] So, Kevin Bacon himself has a Bacon number of 0, every actor who has appeared in a movie with Kevin Bacon has a Bacon number of 1, every actor who has appeared with an actor whose Bacon number is 1 but who is not Kevin Bacon himself has a Bacon number of 2, and so on. For example, Jon Hamm—perhaps best known as Don Draper from the cable television series *Mad Men*—has a Bacon number of 2. Hamm never appeared in a movie with Bacon, but he did have a bit part in the Colin Firth vehicle *A Single Man*, and Firth and Bacon co-starred in Atom Egoyan's *Where the Truth Lies* (Figure 8.1).[3]

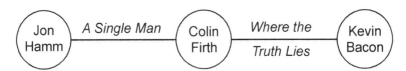

Figure 8.1: A snippet of the movie network, showing that Jon Hamm's Bacon number is at most 2.

---

[1]https://oracleofbacon.org/

[2]The Bacon number is a riff on the older concept of the *Erdös number*, named after the famous mathematician Paul Erdös, which measures the number of degrees of separation from Erdös in the co-authorship graph (where vertices are researchers, and there is an edge between each pair of researchers who have co-authored a paper).

[3]There are also lots of other two-hop paths between Bacon and Hamm.

Shortest paths.   The Bacon number concerns the *shortest* path between two vertices of the movie network, meaning the path using the fewest number of edges. We'll see in Section 8.2 that a graph search strategy known as breadth-first search naturally computes shortest paths. Plenty of other problems boil down to a shortest-path computation, where the definition of "short" depends on the application (minimizing time for driving directions, or money for airline tickets, and so on). Dijkstra's shortest-path algorithm, the subject of Chapter 9, builds on breadth-first search to solve more general shortest-path problems.

Planning.   A path in a graph need not represent a physical path through a physical network. More abstractly, a path is a sequence of decisions taking you from one state to another. Graph search algorithms can be applied to such abstract graphs to compute a plan for reaching a goal state from an initial state. For example, imagine you want to use an algorithm to solve a Sudoku puzzle. Think of the graph where vertices correspond to partially completed Sudoku puzzles (with some of the 81 squares blank, but no rules of Sudoku violated), and directed edges correspond to filling in one new entry of the puzzle (subject to the rules of Sudoku). The problem of computing a solution to the puzzle is exactly the problem of computing a directed path from the vertex corresponding to the initial state of the puzzle to the vertex corresponding to the completed puzzle.[4] For another example, using a robotic hand to grasp a coffee mug is essentially a planning problem. In the associated graph, vertices correspond to the possible configurations of the hand, and edges correspond to small and realizable changes in the configuration.

Connected components.   We'll also see algorithms that build on graph search to compute the connected components (the "pieces") of a graph. Defining and computing the connected components of an undirected graph is relatively easy (Section 8.3). For directed graphs, even defining what a "connected component" should mean is a little subtle. Section 8.6 defines them and shows how to use depth-first search (Section 8.4) to compute them efficiently. We'll also

---

[4]Because this graph is too big to write down explicitly, practical Sudoku solvers incorporate some additional ideas.

see applications of depth-first search to sequencing tasks (Section 8.5) and to understanding the structure of the Web graph (Section 8.7).

8.1.2   For-Free Graph Primitives

The examples in Section 8.1.1 demonstrate that graph search is a fundamental and widely applicable primitive. I'm happy to report that, in this chapter, all our algorithms will be blazingly fast, running in just $O(m + n)$ time, where m and n denote the number of edges and vertices of the graph.[5] That's just a constant factor larger than the amount of time required to read the input![6] We conclude that these algorithms are "for-free primitives"—whenever you have graph data, you should feel free to apply any of these primitives to glean information about what it looks like.[7]

For-Free Primitives

We can think of an algorithm with linear or near-linear running time as a primitive that we can use essentially "for free" because the amount of computation used is barely more than the amount required just to read the input. When you have a primitive relevant to your problem that is so blazingly fast, why not use it? For example, you can always compute the connected components of your graph data in a preprocessing step, even if you're not quite sure how it will help later. One of the goals of this book series is to stock your algorithmic toolbox with as many for-free primitives as possible, ready to be applied at will.

8.1.3   Generic Graph Search

The point of a graph search algorithm is to solve the following problem.

---

[5]Also, the constants hidden in the big-O notation are reasonably small.

[6]In graph search and connectivity problems, there is no reason to expect that the input graph is connected. In the disconnected case, where m might be much smaller than n, the size of a graph is $\Theta(m + n)$ but not necessarily $\Theta(m)$.

[7]Can we do better? No, up to the hidden constant factor: every correct algorithm must at least read the entire input in some cases.

Problem: Graph Search

Input: An undirected or directed graph $G = (V, E)$, and a starting vertex $s \in V$.

Goal: Identify the vertices of V reachable from s in G.

By a vertex v being "reachable," we mean that there is a sequence of edges in G that travels from s to v. If G is a directed graph, all the path's edges should be traversed in the forward (outgoing) direction. For example, in Figure 8.2(a), the set of reachable vertices (from s) is $\{s, u, v, w\}$. In the directed version of the graph in Figure 8.2(b), there is no directed path from s to w, and only the vertices s, u, and v are reachable from s via a directed path.[8]

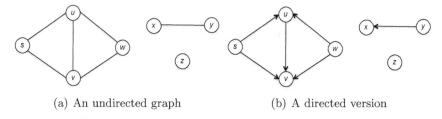

(a) An undirected graph   (b) A directed version

Figure 8.2: In (a), the set of vertices reachable from s is $\{s, u, v, w\}$. In (b), it is $\{s, u, v\}$.

The two graph search strategies that we'll focus on—breadth-first search and depth-first search—are different ways of instantiating a generic graph search algorithm. The generic algorithm systematically finds all the reachable vertices, taking care to avoid exploring anything twice. It maintains an extra variable with each vertex that keeps track of whether or not it has already been explored, planting a flag the first time that vertex is reached. The main loop's responsibility is to reach a new unexplored vertex in each iteration.

---

[8]In general, most of the algorithms and arguments in this chapter apply equally well to undirected and directed graphs. The big exception is computing connected components, which is a trickier problem in directed graphs than in undirected graphs.

GenericSearch

Input: graph $G = (V, E)$ and a vertex $s \in V$.
Postcondition: a vertex is reachable from s if and only if it is marked as "explored."

---

mark s as explored, all other vertices as unexplored
while there is an edge $(v, w) \in E$ with v explored and w unexplored **do**
    choose some such edge (v, w) // `underspecified`
    mark w as explored

The algorithm is essentially the same for both directed and undirected graphs. In the directed case, the edge (v, w) chosen in an iteration of the while loop should be directed from an explored vertex v to an unexplored vertex w.

On Pseudocode

This book series explains algorithms using a mixture of high-level pseudocode and English (as above). I'm assuming that you have the skills to translate such high-level descriptions into working code in your favorite programming language. Several other books and resources on the Web offer concrete implementations of various algorithms in specific programming languages.

The first benefit of emphasizing high-level descriptions over language-specific implementations is flexibility. While I assume familiarity with *some* programming language, I don't care which one. Second, this approach promotes the understanding of algorithms at a deep and conceptual level, unencumbered by low-level details. Seasoned programmers and computer scientists generally think and communicate about algorithms at a similarly high level.

Still, there is no substitute for the detailed understanding of an algorithm that comes from providing your own working implementation of it. I strongly encourage you to implement as many of the algorithms in this book as you have time for. (It's also a great excuse to pick up a new programming language!) For guidance, see the end-of-chapter Programming Problems and supporting test cases.

For example, in the graph in Figure 8.2(a), initially only our home base s is marked as explored. In the first iteration of the while loop, two edges meet the loop condition: (s, u) and (s, v). The GenericSearch algorithm chooses one of these edges—(s, u), say—and marks u as explored. In the second iteration of the loop, there are again two choices: (s, v) and (u, w). The algorithm might choose (u, w), in which case w is marked as explored. With one more iteration (after choosing either (s, v) or (w, v)), v is marked as explored. At this point, the edge (x, y) has two unexplored endpoints and the other edges have two explored endpoints, and the algorithm halts. As one would hope, the vertices marked as explored—s, u, v, and w—are precisely the vertices reachable from s.

This generic graph search algorithm is underspecified, as multiple edges (v, w) can be eligible for selection in an iteration of the while loop. Breadth-first search and depth-first search correspond to two specific decisions about which edge to explore next. No matter how this choice is made, the GenericSearch algorithm is guaranteed to be correct (in both undirected and directed graphs).

Proposition 8.1 (Correctness of Generic Graph Search) *At the conclusion of the GenericSearch algorithm, a vertex $v \in V$ is marked as explored if and only if there is a path from s to v in G.*

Section 8.1.5 provides a formal proof of Proposition 8.1; feel free to skip it if the proposition seems intuitively obvious.

On Lemmas, Theorems, and the Like

In mathematical writing, the most important technical statements are labeled *theorems*. A *lemma* is a technical statement that assists with the proof of a theorem (much as a subroutine assists with the implementation of a larger program). A *corollary* is a statement that follows immediately from an already-proved result, such as a special case of a theorem. We use the term *proposition* for stand-alone technical statements that are not particularly important in their own right.

What about the running time of the `GenericSearch` algorithm? The algorithm explores each edge at most once—after an edge (v, w) has been explored for the first time, both v and w are marked as explored and the edge will not be considered again. This suggests that it should be possible to implement the algorithm in linear time, as long as we can quickly identify an eligible edge (v, w) in each iteration of the while loop. We'll see how this works in detail for breadth-first search and depth-first search in Sections 8.2 and 8.4, respectively.

8.1.4   Breadth-First and Depth-First Search

Every iteration of the `GenericSearch` algorithm chooses an edge that is "on the frontier" of the explored part of the graph, with one endpoint explored and the other unexplored (Figure 8.3). There can be many such edges, and to specify the algorithm fully we need a method for choosing one of them. We'll focus on the two most important strategies: breadth-first search and depth-first search. Both are excellent ways to explore a graph, and each has its own set of applications.

Breadth-first search (BFS). The high-level idea of *breadth-first search*—or *BFS* to its friends—is to explore the vertices of a graph cautiously, in "layers." Layer 0 consists only of the starting vertex s. Layer 1 contains the vertices that neighbor s, meaning the vertices v such that (s, v) is an edge of the graph (directed from s to v, in the case that G is directed). Layer 2 comprises the neighbors of layer-1 vertices that do not already belong to layer 0 or 1, and so on. In Sections 8.2 and 8.3, we'll see:

- how to implement BFS in linear time using a queue (first-in first-out) data structure;

- how to use BFS to compute (in linear time) the length of a shortest path between one vertex and all other vertices, with the

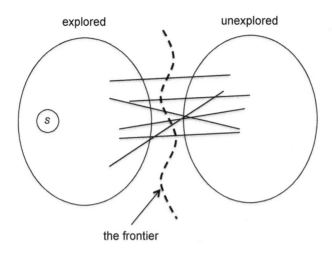

Figure 8.3: Every iteration of the GenericSearch algorithm chooses an edge "on the frontier," with one endpoint explored and the other unexplored.

layer-i vertices being precisely the vertices at distance i from s;

- how to use BFS to compute (in linear time) the connected components of an undirected graph.

Depth-first search (DFS). *Depth-first search—DFS* to its friends—is perhaps even more important. DFS employs a more aggressive strategy for exploring a graph, very much in the spirit of how you might explore a maze, going as deeply as you can and backtracking only when absolutely necessary. In Sections 8.4–8.7, we'll see:

- how to implement DFS in linear time using either recursion or an explicit stack (last-in first-out) data structure;

- how to use DFS to compute (in linear time) a topological ordering of the vertices of a directed acyclic graph, a useful primitive for task sequencing problems;

- how to use DFS to compute (in linear time) the "strongly connected components" of a directed graph, with applications to understanding the structure of the Web.

8.1.5 Correctness of the GenericSearch Algorithm

We now prove Proposition 8.1, which states that at the conclusion of the GenericSearch algorithm with input graph $G = (V, E)$ and starting vertex $s \in V$, a vertex $v \in V$ is marked as explored if and only if there is a path from s to v in G. As usual, if G is a directed graph, the $s \rightsquigarrow v$ path should also be directed, with all edges traversed in the forward direction.

The "only if" direction of the proposition should be intuitively clear: The only way that the GenericSearch algorithm discovers new vertices is by following paths from s.[9]

The "if" direction asserts the less obvious fact that the GenericSearch algorithm doesn't miss anything—it finds every vertex that it could conceivably discover. For this direction, we'll use a proof by contradiction. Recall that in this type of proof, you assume the *opposite* of what you want to prove, and then build on this assumption with a sequence of logically correct steps that culminates in a patently false statement. Such a contradiction implies that the assumption can't be true, which proves the desired statement.

So, assume that there is a path from s to v in the graph G, but the GenericSearch algorithm somehow misses it and concludes with the vertex v marked as unexplored. Let $S \subseteq V$ denote the vertices of G marked as explored by the algorithm. The vertex s belongs to S (by the first line of the algorithm), and the vertex v does not (by assumption). Because the $s \rightsquigarrow v$ path travels from a vertex inside S to one outside S, at least one edge e of the path has one endpoint u in S and the other w outside S (with e directed from u to w in the case that G is directed); see Figure 8.4. But this, my friends, is impossible: The edge e would be eligible for selection in the while loop of the GenericSearch algorithm, and the algorithm would have explored at least one more vertex, rather than giving up! There's no way that the GenericSearch algorithm could have halted at this point, so we've reached a contradiction. This contradiction concludes the proof of Proposition 8.1. $\mathcal{QED}$[10]

---

[9]If we wanted to be pedantic about it, we'd prove this direction by induction on the number of loop iterations.

[10]"Q.e.d." is an abbreviation for *quod erat demonstrandum*, and means "that which was to be demonstrated." In mathematical writing, it is used at the end of a proof to mark its completion.

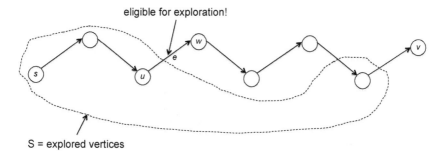

S = explored vertices

Figure 8.4: Proof of Proposition 8.1. As long as the GenericSearch algorithm has not yet discovered all the reachable vertices, there is an eligible edge along which it can explore further.

8.2   Breadth-First Search and Shortest Paths

Let's drill down on our first specific graph search strategy, *breadth-first search*.

8.2.1   High-Level Idea

Breadth-first search explores the vertices of a graph in layers, in order of increasing distance from the starting vertex. Layer 0 contains the starting vertex s and nothing else. Layer 1 is the set of vertices that are one hop away from s—that is, s's neighbors. These are the vertices that are explored immediately after s in breadth-first search. For example, in the graph in Figure 8.5, a and b are the neighbors of s and constitute layer 1. In general, the vertices in a layer i are those that neighbor a vertex in layer $i-1$ and that do not already belong to one of the layers $0, 1, 2, \ldots, i-1$. Breadth-first search explores all of layer-i vertices immediately after completing its exploration of layer-$(i-1)$ vertices. (Vertices not reachable from s do not belong to any layer.) For example, in Figure 8.5, the layer-2 vertices are c and d, as they neighbor layer-1 vertices but do not themselves belong to layer 0 or 1. (The vertex s is also a neighbor of a layer-1 vertex, but it already belongs to layer 0.) The last layer of the graph in Figure 8.5 comprises only the vertex e.

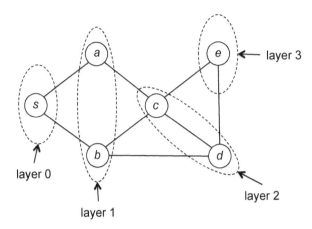

Figure 8.5: Breadth-first search discovers vertices in layers. The layer-i vertices are the neighbors of the layer-$(i-1)$ vertices that do not appear in any earlier layer.

Quiz 8.1

Consider an undirected graph with $n \geq 2$ vertices. What are the minimum and maximum number of different layers that the graph could have, respectively?

a) 1 and $n - 1$

b) 2 and $n - 1$

c) 1 and n

d) 2 and n

(See Section 8.2.6 for the solution and discussion.)

8.2.2   Pseudocode for BFS

Implementing breadth-first search in linear time requires a simple "first-in first-out" data structure known as a *queue*. BFS uses a queue to keep track of which vertices to explore next. If you're unfamiliar with queues, now is a good time to read up on them in your favorite introductory programming book (or on Wikipedia). The gist is that a queue is a data structure for maintaining a list of objects, and you can remove stuff from the front or add stuff to the back in constant time.[11]

BFS

Input: graph $G = (V, E)$ in adjacency-list representation, and a vertex $s \in V$.
Postcondition: a vertex is reachable from s if and only if it is marked as "explored."

---

1 mark s as explored, all other vertices as unexplored
2 $Q :=$ a queue data structure, initialized with s
3 **while** Q is not empty **do**
4   remove the vertex from the front of Q, call it v
5   **for** each edge (v, w) in v's adjacency list **do**
6   **if** w is unexplored **then**
7   mark w as explored
8   add w to the end of Q

Each iteration of the while loop explores one new vertex. In line 5, BFS iterates through all the edges incident to the vertex v (if G is undirected) or through all the outgoing edges from v (if G is directed).[12] Unexplored neighbors of v are added to the end of the queue and are marked as explored; they will eventually be processed in later iterations of the algorithm.

8.2.3   An Example

Let's see how our pseudocode works for the graph in Figure 8.5, numbering the vertices in order of insertion into the queue (equivalently, in order of exploration). The starting vertex s is always the first to

---

[11]You may never need to implement a queue from scratch, as they are built in to most modern programming languages. If you do, you can use a doubly linked list. Or, if you have advance knowledge of the maximum number of objects that you might have to store (which is $|V|$, in the case of BFS), you can get away with a fixed-length array and a couple of indices (which keep track of the front and back of the queue).

[12]This is the step where it's so convenient to have the input graph represented via adjacency lists.

be explored. The first iteration of the while loop extracts s from the queue Q and the subsequent for loop examines the edges (s, a) and (s, b), in whatever order these edges appear in s's adjacency list. Because neither a nor b is marked as explored, both get inserted into the queue. Let's say that edge (s, a) came first and so a is inserted before b. The current state of the graph and the queue is now:

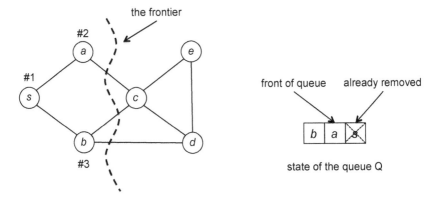

The next iteration of the while loop extracts the vertex a from the front of the queue, and considers its incident edges (s, a) and (a, c). It skips over the former after double-checking that s is already marked as explored, and adds the (previously unexplored) vertex c to the end of the queue. The third iteration extracts the vertex b from the front of the queue and adds vertex d to the end (because s and c are already marked as explored, they are skipped over). The new picture is:

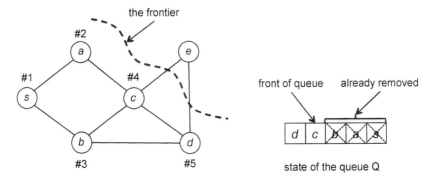

In the fourth iteration, the vertex c is removed from the front of the queue. Of its neighbors, the vertex e is the only one not encountered before, and it is added to the end of the queue. The final two iterations extract d and then e from the queue, and verify that all of their neighbors have already been explored. The queue is then empty, and the algorithm halts. The vertices are explored in order of the layers, with the layer-i vertices explored immediately after the layer-$(i - 1)$ vertices (Figure 8.6).

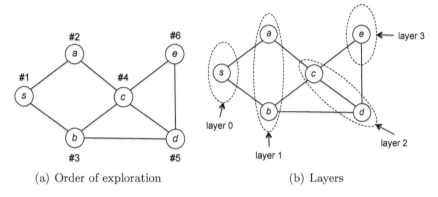

(a) Order of exploration   (b) Layers

Figure 8.6: In breadth-first search, the layer-i vertices are explored immediately after the layer-$(i - 1)$ vertices.

8.2.4 Correctness and Running Time

Breadth-first search discovers all the vertices reachable from the starting vertex, and it runs in linear time. The more refined running time bound in Theorem 8.2(c) below will come in handy for our linear-time algorithm for computing connected components (described in Section 8.3).

Theorem 8.2 (Properties of BFS) *For every undirected or directed graph $G = (V, E)$ in adjacency-list representation and for every starting vertex $s \in V$:*

(a) At the conclusion of BFS, a vertex $v \in V$ is marked as explored if and only if there is a path from s to v in G.

(b) The running time of BFS is $O(m + n)$, where $m = |E|$ and $n = |V|$.

(c) The running time of lines 2–8 of BFS is

$$O(m_s + n_s),$$

where m_s and n_s denote the number of edges and vertices, respectively, reachable from s in G.

Proof: Part (a) follows from the guarantee in Proposition 8.1 for the generic graph search algorithm GenericSearch, of which BFS is a special case.[13] Part (b) follows from part (c), as the overall running time of BFS is just the running time of lines 2–8 plus the $O(n)$ time needed for the initialization in line 1.

We can prove part (c) by inspecting the pseudocode. The initialization in line 2 takes $O(1)$ time. In the main while loop, the algorithm only ever encounters the n_s vertices that are reachable from s. Because no vertex is explored twice, each such vertex is added to the end of the queue and removed from the front of the queue exactly once. Each of these operations takes $O(1)$ time—this is the whole point of the first-in first-out queue data structure—and so the total amount of time spent in lines 3–4 and 7–8 is $O(n_s)$. Each of the m_s edges (v, w) reachable from s is processed in line 5 at most twice—once when v is explored, and once when w is explored.[14] Thus the total amount of time spent in lines 5–6 is $O(m_s)$, and the overall running time for lines 2–8 is $O(m_s + n_s)$. *QED*

8.2.5   Shortest Paths

The properties in Theorem 8.2 are not unique to breadth-first search—for example, they also hold for depth-first search. What *is* unique about BFS is that, with just a couple extra lines of code, it efficiently computes shortest-path distances.

---

[13]Formally, BFS is equivalent to the version of GenericSearch where, in every iteration of the latter's while loop, the algorithm chooses the eligible edge (v, w) for which v was discovered the earliest, breaking ties among v's eligible edges according to their order in v's adjacency list. If that sounds too complicated, you can alternatively check that the proof of Proposition 8.1 holds verbatim also for breadth-first search. Intuitively, breadth-first search discovers vertices only by exploring paths from s; as long as it hasn't explored every vertex on a path, the "next vertex" on the path is still in the queue awaiting future exploration.

[14]If G is a directed graph, each edge is processed at most once, when its tail vertex is explored.

Problem Definition

In a graph G, we use the notation $dist(v, w)$ for the fewest number of edges in a path from v to w (or $+\infty$, if G contains no path from v to w).[15]

Problem: Shortest Paths (Unit Edge Lengths)

Input: An undirected or directed graph $G = (V, E)$, and a starting vertex $s \in V$.

Output: $dist(s, v)$ for every vertex $v \in V$.[16]

For example, if G is the movie network and s is the vertex corresponding to Kevin Bacon, the problem of computing shortest paths is precisely the problem of computing everyone's Bacon number (Section 8.1.1). The basic graph search problem (Section 8.1.3) corresponds to the special case of identifying all the vertices v with $dist(s, v) \neq +\infty$.

Pseudocode

To compute shortest paths, we add two lines to the basic BFS algorithm (lines 2 and 9 below); these increase the algorithm's running time by a small constant factor. The first one initializes preliminary estimates of vertices' shortest-path distances—0 for s, and $+\infty$ for the other vertices, which might not even be reachable from s. The second one executes whenever a vertex w is discovered for the first time, and computes w's final shortest-path distance as one more than that of the vertex v that triggered w's discovery.

---

[15] As usual, if G is directed, all the edges of the path should be traversed in the forward direction.

[16] The phrase "unit edge lengths" in the problem statement refers to the assumption that each edge of G contributes 1 to the length of a path. Chapter 9 generalizes BFS to compute shortest paths in graphs in which each edge has its own nonnegative length.

Augmented-BFS

Input: graph $G = (V, E)$ in adjacency-list representation, and a vertex $s \in V$.
Postcondition: for every vertex $v \in V$, the value $l(v)$ equals the true shortest-path distance $dist(s, v)$.

1   mark s as explored, all other vertices as unexplored
2   $l(s) := 0$, $l(v) := +\infty$ for every $v \neq s$
3   $Q :=$ a queue data structure, initialized with s
4   **while** Q is not empty **do**
5   remove the vertex from the front of Q, call it v
6   **for** each edge (v, w) in v's adjacency list **do**
7   **if** w is unexplored **then**
8   mark w as explored
9               $l(w) := l(v) + 1$
10   add w to the end of Q

Example and Analysis

In our running example (Figure 8.6), the first iteration of the while loop discovers the vertices a and b. Because s triggered their discovery and $l(s) = 0$, the algorithm reassigns $l(a)$ and $l(b)$ from $+\infty$ to 1:

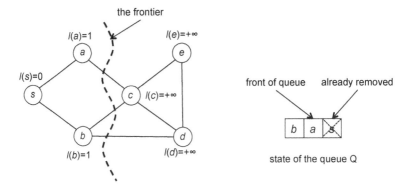

The second iteration of the while loop processes the vertex a, leading to c's discovery. The algorithm reassigns $l(c)$ from $+\infty$ to $l(a) + 1$, which is 2. Similarly, in the third iteration, $l(d)$ is set to $l(b) + 1$, which is also 2:

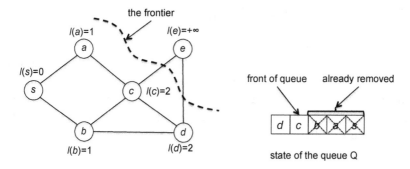

The fourth iteration discovers the final vertex e via the vertex c, and sets $l(e)$ to $l(c) + 1$, which is 3. At this point, for every vertex v, $l(v)$ equals the true shortest-path distance $dist(s, v)$, which also equals the number of the layer that contains v (Figure 8.6). These properties hold in general, and not just for this example.

Theorem 8.3 (Properties of Augmented-BFS) *For every undirected or directed graph $G = (V, E)$ in adjacency-list representation and for every starting vertex $s \in V$:*

(a) *At the conclusion of* Augmented-BFS, *for every vertex $v \in V$, the value of $l(v)$ equals the length $dist(s, v)$ of a shortest path from s to v in G (or $+\infty$, if no such path exists).*

(b) *The running time of* Augmented-BFS *is $O(m+n)$, where $m = |E|$ and $n = |V|$.*

Because the asymptotic running time of the Augmented-BFS algorithm is the same as that of BFS, part (b) of Theorem 8.3 follows from the latter's running time guarantee (Theorem 8.2(b)). Part (a) follows from two observations. First, the vertices v with $dist(s, v) = i$ are precisely the vertices in the ith layer of the graph—this is why we defined layers the way we did. Second, for every layer-i vertex w, Augmented-BFS eventually sets $l(w) = i$ (since w is discovered via a layer-$(i-1)$ vertex v with $l(v) = i - 1$). For vertices not in any layer—that is, not reachable from s—both $dist(s, v)$ and $l(v)$ are $+\infty$.[17]

---

[17]If you're hungry for a more rigorous proof, then proceed—in the privacy of your own home—by induction on the number of while loop iterations performed by the Augmented-BFS algorithm. Alternatively, Theorem 8.3(a) is a special case of the correctness of Dijkstra's shortest-path algorithm, as proved in Section 9.3.

8.2.6   Solution to Quiz 8.1

Correct answer: (d). An undirected graph with $n \geq 2$ vertices has at least two layers and at most n layers. When $n \geq 2$, there cannot be fewer than two layers because s is the only vertex in layer 0. Complete graphs have only two layers (Figure 8.7(a)). There cannot be more than n layers, as layers are disjoint and contain at least one vertex each. Path graphs have n layers (Figure 8.7(b)).

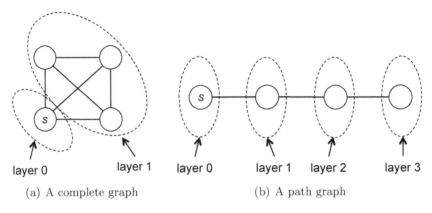

layer 0	layer 1	layer 0	layer 1	layer 2	layer 3

(a) A complete graph   (b) A path graph

Figure 8.7: An n-vertex graph can have anywhere from two to n different layers.

8.3   Computing Connected Components

In this section, $G = (V, E)$ will always denote an *undirected* graph. We postpone the more difficult connectivity problems in directed graphs until Section 8.6.

8.3.1   Connected Components

An undirected graph $G = (V, E)$ naturally falls into "pieces," which are called *connected components* (Figure 8.8). More formally, a connected component is a maximal subset $S \subseteq V$ of vertices such that there is a path from any vertex in S to any other vertex in S.[18] For example,

---

[18]Still more formally, the connected components of a graph can be defined as the *equivalence classes* of a suitable *equivalence relation*. Equivalence relations are usually covered in a first course on proofs or on discrete mathematics. A

the connected components of the graph in Figure 8.8 are $\{1, 3, 5, 7, 9\}$, $\{2, 4\}$, and $\{6, 8, 10\}$.

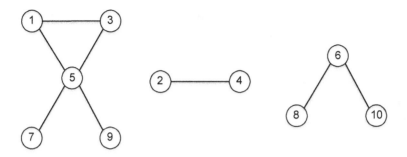

Figure 8.8: A graph with vertex set $\{1, 2, 3, \dots, 10\}$ and three connected components.

The goal of this section is to use breadth-first search to compute the connected components of a graph in linear time.[19]

Problem: Undirected Connected Components

Input: An undirected graph $G = (V, E)$.

Goal: Identify the connected components of G.

Next, let's double-check your understanding of the definition of connected components.

---

relation on a set X of objects specifies, for each pair $x, y \in X$ of objects, whether or not x and y are related. (If so, we write $x \sim y$.) For connected components, the relevant relation (on the set V) is "$v \sim_G w$ if and only if there is a path between v and w in G." An *equivalence* relation satisfies three properties. First, it is *reflexive*, meaning that $x \sim x$ for every $x \in X$. (Satisfied by $\sim_G$, as the empty path connects a vertex with itself.) Second, it is *symmetric*, with $x \sim y$ if and only if $y \sim x$. (Satisfied by $\sim_G$, as G is undirected.) Finally, it is *transitive*, meaning that $x \sim y$ and $y \sim z$ implies that $x \sim z$. (Satisfied by $\sim_G$, as you can paste together a path between vertices u and v with a path between vertices v and w to get a path between u and w.) An equivalence relation partitions the set of objects into equivalence classes, with each object related to all the objects in its class, and only to these. The equivalence classes of the relation $\sim_G$ are the connected components of G.

[19]Other graph search algorithms, including depth-first search, can be used to compute connected components in exactly the same way.

Quiz 8.2

Consider an undirected graph with n vertices and m edges. What are the minimum and maximum number of connected components that the graph could have, respectively?

a) 1 and $n - 1$

b) 1 and n

c) 1 and $\max\{m, n\}$

d) 2 and $\max\{m, n\}$

(See Section 8.3.6 for the solution and discussion.)

8.3.2   Applications

There are several reasons why you might be interested in the connected components of a graph.

Detecting network failures.   One obvious application is checking whether or not a network, such as a road or communication network, has become disconnected.

Data visualization.   Another application is in graph visualization— if you're trying to draw or otherwise visualize a graph, presumably you want to display the different components separately.

Clustering.   Suppose you have a collection of objects that you care about, with each pair annotated as either "similar" or "dissimilar." For example, the objects could be documents (like crawled Web pages or news stories), with similar objects corresponding to near-duplicate documents (perhaps differing only in a timestamp or a headline). Or the objects could be genomes, with two genomes deemed similar if a small number of mutations can transform one into the other.

Now form an undirected graph $G = (V, E)$, with vertices corresponding to objects and edges corresponding to pairs of similar objects. Intuitively, each connected component of this graph represents a set of objects that share much in common. For example, if the objects are crawled news stories, one might expect the vertices of a connected component to be variations on the same story reported on different

Web sites. If the objects are genomes, a connected component might correspond to different individuals belonging to the same species.

8.3.3   The UCC Algorithm

Computing the connected components of an undirected graph easily reduces to breadth-first search (or other graph search algorithms, such as depth-first search). The idea is to use an outer loop to make a single pass over the vertices, invoking BFS as a subroutine whenever the algorithm encounters a vertex that it has never seen before. This outer loop ensures that the algorithm looks at every vertex at least once. Vertices are initialized as unexplored before the outer loop, and not inside a call to BFS. The algorithm also maintains a field $cc(v)$ for each vertex v, to remember which connected component contains it. By identifying each vertex of V with its position in the vertex array, we can assume that $V = \{1, 2, 3, \ldots, n\}$.

UCC

Input: undirected graph $G = (V, E)$ in adjacency-list representation, with $V = \{1, 2, 3, \ldots, n\}$.
Postcondition: for every $u, v \in V$, $cc(u) = cc(v)$ if and only if u, v are in the same connected component.

---

mark all vertices as unexplored
$numCC := 0$
for $i := 1$ to n **do**   // try all vertices
   if i is unexplored **then**   // avoid redundancy
      $numCC := numCC + 1$ // new component
      // call BFS starting at i (lines 2-8)
      $Q :=$ a queue data structure, initialized with i
      while Q is not empty **do**
         remove the vertex from the front of Q, call it v
         $cc(v) := numCC$
         for each (v, w) in v's adjacency list **do**
            if w is unexplored **then**
               mark w as explored
               add w to the end of Q

8.3.4   An Example

Let's trace the UCC algorithm's execution on the graph in Figure 8.8. The algorithm marks all vertices as unexplored and starts the outer for loop with vertex 1. This vertex has not been seen before, so the algorithm invokes BFS from it. Because BFS finds everything reachable from its starting vertex (Theorem 8.2(a)), it discovers all the vertices in $\{1, 3, 5, 7, 9\}$, and sets their cc-values to 1. One possible order of exploration is:

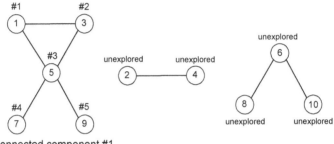

Once this call to BFS completes, the algorithm's outer for loop marches on and considers vertex 2. This vertex was not discovered by the first call to BFS, so BFS is invoked again, this time with vertex 2 as the starting vertex. After discovering vertices 2 and 4 (and setting their cc-values to 2), this call to BFS completes and the UCC algorithm resumes its outer for loop. Has the algorithm seen vertex 3 before? Yup, in the first BFS call. What about vertex 4? Yes again, this time in the second BFS call. Vertex 5? Been there, done that in the first BFS call. But what about vertex 6? Neither of the previous BFS calls discovered this vertex, so BFS is called again with vertex 6 as the starting vertex. This third call to BFS discovers the vertices in $\{6, 8, 10\}$, and sets their cc-values to 3:

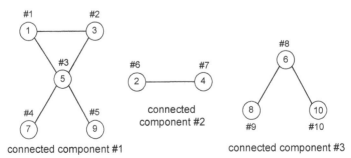

Finally, the algorithm verifies that the remaining vertices (7, 8, 9, and 10) have already been explored and halts.

8.3.5   Correctness and Running Time

The UCC algorithm correctly computes the connected components of an undirected graph, and does so in linear time.

Theorem 8.4 (Properties of UCC) *For every undirected graph* $G = (V, E)$ *in adjacency-list representation:*

(a) *At the conclusion of* UCC, *for every pair* u, v *of vertices,* $cc(u) = cc(v)$ *if and only if* u *and* v *belong to the same connected component of* G.

(b) *The running time of* UCC *is* $O(m + n)$, *where* $m = |E|$ *and* $n = |V|$.

Proof: For correctness, the first property of breadth-first search (Theorem 8.2(a)) implies that each call to BFS with a starting vertex i will discover the vertices in i's connected component and nothing more. The UCC algorithm gives these vertices a common cc-value. Because no vertex is explored twice, each call to BFS identifies a new connected component, with each component having a different cc-value. The outer for loop ensures that every vertex is visited at least once, so the algorithm will discover every connected component.

The running time bound follows from our refined running time analysis of BFS (Theorem 8.2(c)). Each call to BFS from a vertex i runs in $O(m_i + n_i)$ time, where m_i and n_i denote the number of edges and vertices, respectively, in i's connected component. As BFS is called only once for each connected component, and each vertex or edge of G participates in exactly one component, the combined running time of all the BFS calls is $O(\sum_i m_i + \sum_i n_i) = O(m+n)$. The initialization and additional bookkeeping performed by the algorithm requires only $O(n)$ time, so the final running time is $O(m+n)$. *QED*

8.3.6   Solution to Quiz 8.2

Correct answer: (b). A graph with one connected component is one in which you can get from anywhere to anywhere else. Path graphs and complete graphs (Figure 8.7) are two examples. At the other extreme, in a graph with no edges, each vertex is in its own connected component, for a total of n. There cannot be more than n connected components, as they are disjoint and each contains at least one vertex.

8.4   Depth-First Search

Why do we need another graph search strategy? After all, breadth-first search seems pretty awesome—it finds all the vertices reachable from the starting vertex in linear time, and can even compute shortest-path distances along the way.

There's another linear-time graph search strategy, *depth-first search (DFS)*, which comes with its own impressive catalog of applications (not already covered by BFS). For example, we'll see how to use DFS to compute in linear time a topological ordering of the vertices of a directed acyclic graph, as well as the connected components (appropriately defined) of a directed graph.

8.4.1   An Example

If breadth-first search is the cautious and tentative exploration strategy, depth-first search is its more aggressive cousin, always exploring from the most recently discovered vertex and backtracking only when necessary (like exploring a maze). Before we describe the full pseudocode for DFS, let's illustrate how it works on the same running example used in Section 8.2 (Figure 8.9).

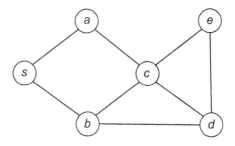

Figure 8.9: Running example for depth-first search.

Like BFS, DFS marks a vertex as explored the first time it discovers it. Because it begins its exploration at the starting vertex s, for the graph in Figure 8.9, the first iteration of DFS examines the edges (s, a) and (s, b), in whatever order these edges appear in s's adjacency list. Let's say (s, a) comes first, leading DFS to discover the vertex a and mark it as explored. The second iteration of DFS is where it diverges from BFS—rather than considering next s's other layer-1 neighbor b, DFS immediately proceeds to exploring the neighbors of a. (It will eventually get back to exploring (s, b).) Perhaps from a it checks s first (which is already marked as explored) and then discovers the vertex c, which is where it travels next:

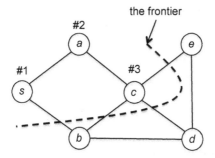

Then DFS examines in some order the neighbors of c, the most recently discovered vertex. To keep things interesting, let's say that DFS discovers d next, followed by e:

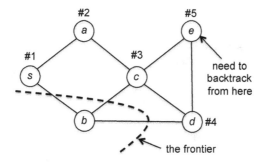

From e, DFS has nowhere to go—both of e's neighbors are already marked as explored. DFS is forced to retreat to the previous vertex, namely d, and resume exploring the rest of its neighbors. From d, DFS will discover the final vertex b (perhaps after checking c and finding it marked as explored). Once at b, the dominoes fall quickly. DFS discovers that all of b's neighbors have already been explored, and must backtrack to the previously visited vertex, which is d. Similarly, because all of d's remaining neighbors are already marked as explored, DFS must rewind further, to c. DFS then retreats further to a (after checking that all of c's remaining neighbors are marked as explored), then to s. It finally stops once it checks s's remaining neighbor (which is b) and finds it marked as explored.

8.4.2   Pseudocode for DFS

Iterative Implementation

One way to think about and implement DFS is to start from the code for BFS and make two changes: (i) swap in a stack data structure (which is last-in first-out) for the queue (which is first-in first-out); and (ii) postpone checking whether a vertex has already been explored until after removing it from the data structure.[20,21]

DFS (Iterative Version)

Input: graph $G = (V, E)$ in adjacency-list representation, and a vertex $s \in V$.
Postcondition: a vertex is reachable from s if and only if it is marked as "explored."

---

mark all vertices as unexplored
$S :=$ a stack data structure, initialized with s
while S is not empty **do**
    remove ("pop") the vertex v from the front of S
    if v is unexplored **then**
        mark v as explored
        for each edge (v, w) in v's adjacency list **do**
            add ("push") w to the front of S

---

[20] A *stack* is a "last-in first-out" data structure—like those stacks of upside-down trays at a cafeteria—that is typically studied in a first programming course (along with queues, see footnote 11). A stack maintains a list of objects, and you can add an object to the beginning of the list (a "push") or remove one from the beginning of the list (a "pop") in constant time.

[21] Would the algorithm behave the same if we made only the first change?

As usual, the edges processed in the for loop are the edges incident to v (if G is an undirected graph) or the edges outgoing from v (if G is a directed graph).

For example, in the graph in Figure 8.9, the first iteration of DFS's while loop pops the vertex s and pushes its two neighbors onto the stack in some order, say, with b first and a second. Because a was the last to be pushed, it is the first to be popped, in the second iteration of the while loop. This causes s and c to be pushed onto the stack, let's say with c first. The vertex s is popped in the next iteration; since it has already been marked as explored, the algorithm skips it. Then c is popped, and all of its neighbors (a, b, d, and e) are pushed onto the stack, joining the first occurrence of b. If d is pushed last, and also b is pushed before e when d is popped in the next iteration, then we recover the order of exploration from Section 8.4.1 (as you should check).

Recursive Implementation

Depth-first search also has an elegant recursive implementation.[22]

DFS (Recursive Version)

Input: graph $G = (V, E)$ in adjacency-list representation, and a vertex $s \in V$.
Postcondition: a vertex is reachable from s if and only if it is marked as "explored."

```
// all vertices unexplored before outer call
mark s as explored
for each edge (s, v) in s's adjacency list do
    if v is unexplored then
        DFS (G, v)
```

In this implementation, all recursive calls to DFS have access to the same set of global variables which track the vertices that have been marked as explored (with all vertices initially unexplored). The aggressive nature of DFS is perhaps more obvious in this implementation—the

---

[22]I'm assuming you've heard of recursion as part of your programming background. A recursive procedure is one that invokes itself as a subroutine.

algorithm immediately recurses on the first unexplored neighbor that it finds, before considering the remaining neighbors.[23] In effect, the explicit stack data structure in the iterative implementation of DFS is being simulated by the program stack of recursive calls in the recursive implementation.[24]

8.4.3   Correctness and Running Time

Depth-first search is just as correct and just as blazingly fast as breadth-first search, for the same reasons (cf., Theorem 8.2).[25]

Theorem 8.5 (Properties of DFS) *For every undirected or directed graph $G = (V, E)$ in adjacency-list representation and for every starting vertex $s \in V$:*

(a) *At the conclusion of DFS, a vertex $v \in V$ is marked as explored if and only if there is a path from s to v in G.*

(b) *The running time of DFS is $O(m + n)$, where $m = |E|$ and $n = |V|$.*

Part (a) holds because depth-first search is a special case of the generic graph search algorithm `GenericSearch` (see Proposition 8.1).[26] Part (b) holds because DFS examines each edge at most twice (once from each endpoint) and, because the stack supports pushes and pops in $O(1)$ time, performs a constant number of operations per edge examination (for $O(m)$ total). The initialization requires $O(n)$ time.[27]

---

[23] As stated, the two versions of DFS explore the edges in a vertex's adjacency list in opposite orders. (Do you see why?) If one of the versions is modified to iterate backward through a vertex's adjacency list, then the iterative and recursive implementations explore the vertices in the same order.

[24] Pro tip: If your computer runs out of memory while executing the recursive version of DFS on a big graph, you should either switch to the iterative version or increase the program stack size in your programming environment.

[25] The abbreviation "cf." stands for *confer* and means "compare to."

[26] Formally, DFS is equivalent to the version of `GenericSearch` in which, in every iteration of the latter's while loop, the algorithm chooses the eligible edge (v, w) for which v was discovered most recently. Ties among v's eligible edges are broken according to their order (for the recursive version) or their reverse order (for the iterative version) in v's adjacency list.

[27] The refined bound in Theorem 8.2(c) also holds for DFS (for the same reasons), which means DFS can substitute for BFS in the linear-time UCC algorithm for computing connected components in Section 8.3.

8.5 Topological Sort

Depth-first search is perfectly suited for computing a topological ordering of a directed acyclic graph. "What's that and who cares," you say?

8.5.1 Topological Orderings

Imagine that you have a bunch of tasks to complete, and there are *precedence constraints*, meaning that you cannot start some of the tasks until you have completed others. Think, for example, about the courses in a university degree program, some of which are prerequisites for others. One application of topological orderings is to sequencing tasks so that all precedence constraints are respected.

Topological Orderings

Let $G = (V, E)$ be a directed graph. A *topological ordering* of G is an assignment $f(v)$ of every vertex $v \in V$ to a different number such that:

for every $(v, w) \in E$, $f(v) < f(w)$.

The function f effectively orders the vertices, from the vertex with the smallest f-value to the one with the largest. The condition asserts that all of G's (directed) edges should travel forward in the ordering, with the label of the tail of an edge smaller than that of its head.

Quiz 8.3

How many different topological orderings does the following graph have? Use only the labels $\{1, 2, 3, 4\}$.

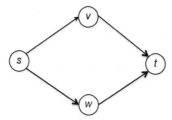

a) 0

b) 1

c) 2

d) 3

(See Section 8.5.7 for the solution and discussion.)

You can visualize a topological ordering by plotting the vertices in order of their f-values. In a topological ordering, all edges of the graph are directed from left to right. Figure 8.10 plots the topological orderings identified in the solution to Quiz 8.3.

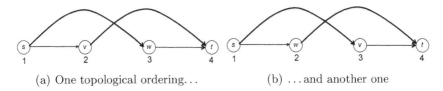

(a) One topological ordering...   (b) ...and another one

Figure 8.10: A topological ordering effectively plots the vertices of a graph on a line, with all edges going from left to right.

When the vertices of a graph represent tasks and the directed edges represent precedence constraints, topological orderings correspond exactly to the different ways to sequence the tasks while respecting the precedence constraints.

8.5.2   When Does a Topological Ordering Exist?

Does every graph have a topological ordering? No way. Think about a graph consisting solely of a directed cycle (Figure 8.11(a)). No matter what vertex ordering you choose, traversing the edges of the cycle takes you back to the starting point, which is possible only if some edges go backward in the ordering (Figure 8.11(b)).

More generally, it is impossible to topologically order the vertices of a graph that contains a directed cycle. Equivalently, it is impossible to sequence a set of tasks when their dependencies are circular.

Happily, directed cycles are the only obstruction to topological orderings. A directed graph without any directed cycles is called—

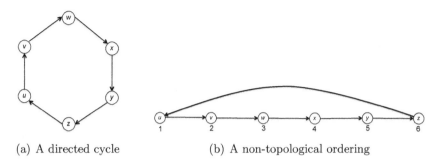

(a) A directed cycle   (b) A non-topological ordering

Figure 8.11: Only a graph without directed cycles can have a topological ordering.

wait for it—a *directed acyclic graph*, or simply a *DAG*. For example, the graph in Figure 8.10 is directed acyclic; the graph in Figure 8.11 is not.

Theorem 8.6 (Every DAG Has a Topological Ordering)
Every directed acyclic graph has at least one topological ordering.

To prove this theorem, we'll need the following lemma about source vertices. A *source vertex* of a directed graph is a vertex with no incoming edges. (Analogously, a *sink vertex* is one with no outgoing edges.) For example, s is the unique source vertex in the graph in Figure 8.10; the directed cycle in Figure 8.11 does not have any source vertices.

Lemma 8.7 (Every DAG Has a Source) *Every directed acyclic graph has at least one source vertex.*

Lemma 8.7 is true because if you keep following incoming edges backward out of an arbitrary vertex of a directed acyclic graph, you're bound to eventually reach a source vertex. (Otherwise, you would produce a cycle, which is impossible.) See also Figure 8.12.[28]

---

[28]More formally, pick a vertex v_0 of a directed acyclic graph G; if it's a source vertex, we're done. If not, it has at least one incoming edge (v_1, v_0). If v_1 is a source vertex, we're done. Otherwise, there is an incoming edge of the form (v_2, v_1) and we can iterate again. After iterating up to n times, where n is the number of vertices, we either find a source vertex or produce a sequence of n edges $(v_n, v_{n-1}), (v_{n-1}, v_{n-2}), \ldots, (v_1, v_0)$. Because there are only n vertices, there's at

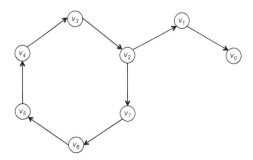

Figure 8.12: Tracing incoming edges back from a vertex fails to find a source vertex only if the graph contains a directed cycle.

We can prove Theorem 8.6 by populating a topological ordering from left to right with successively extracted source vertices.[29]

Proof of Theorem 8.6: Let G be a directed acyclic graph with n vertices. The plan is to assign f-values to vertices in increasing order, from 1 to n. Which vertex has earned the right to wear 1 as its f-value? It had better be a source vertex—if a vertex with an incoming edge was assigned the first position, the incoming edge would go backward in the ordering. So, let v_1 be a source vertex of G—one exists by Lemma 8.7—and assign $f(v_1) = 1$. If there are multiple source vertices, pick one arbitrarily.

Next, obtain the graph G' from G by removing v_1 and all its edges. Because G is directed acyclic, so is G'—deleting stuff can't create new cycles. We can therefore recursively compute a topological ordering of G', using the labels $\{2, 3, 4, \ldots, n\}$, with every edge in G' traveling forward in the ordering. (Since each recursive call is on a smaller graph, the recursion eventually stops.) The only edges in G that are not also in G' are the (outgoing) edges of v_1; as $f(v_1) = 1$, these also travel forward in the ordering.[30] $\mathcal{QED}$

least one repeat vertex in the sequence $v_n, v_{n-1}, \ldots, v_0$. But if $v_j = v_i$ with $j > i$, then the edges $(v_j, v_{j-1}), \ldots, (v_{i+1}, v_i)$ form a directed cycle, contradicting the assumption that G is directed acyclic. (In Figure 8.12, $i = 2$ and $j = 8$.)

[29]Alternatively, following outgoing edges rather than incoming edges in the proof of Lemma 8.7 shows that every DAG has at least one sink vertex, and we can populate a topological ordering from right to left with successively extracted sink vertices.

[30]If you prefer a formal proof of correctness, proceed in the privacy of your

8.5.3   Computing a Topological Ordering

Theorem 8.6 implies that it makes sense to ask for a topological ordering of a directed graph if and only if the graph is directed acyclic.

Problem: Topological Sort

Input: A directed acyclic graph $G = (V, E)$.

Output: A topological ordering of the vertices of G.

The proofs of Lemma 8.7 and Theorem 8.6 naturally lead to an algorithm. For an n-vertex directed acyclic graph in adjacency-list representation, the former proof gives an $O(n)$-time subroutine for finding a source vertex. The latter proof computes a topological ordering with n invocations of this subroutine, plucking off a new source vertex in each iteration.[31] The running time of this algorithm is $O(n^2)$, which is linear time for the densest graphs (with $m = \Theta(n^2)$ edges) but not for sparser graphs (where n^2 could be way bigger than m). Next up: a slicker solution via depth-first search, resulting in a linear-time $(O(m + n))$ algorithm.[32]

8.5.4   Topological Sort via DFS

The slick way to compute a topological ordering is to augment depth-first search in two small ways. For simplicity, we'll start from the recursive implementation of DFS in Section 8.4. The first addition is an outer loop that makes a single pass over the vertices, invoking DFS as a subroutine whenever a previously unexplored vertex is discovered. This ensures that every vertex is eventually discovered and assigned a label. The global variable *curLabel* keeps track of where we are in the topological ordering. Our algorithm will compute an ordering in reverse order (from right to left), so *curLabel* counts down from the number of vertices to 1.

---

own home by induction on the number of vertices.

[31] For the graph in Figure 8.10, this algorithm might compute either of the two topological orderings, depending on which of v, w is chosen as the source vertex in the second iteration, after s has been removed.

[32] With some cleverness, the algorithm implicit in the proofs of Lemma 8.7 and Theorem 8.6 can also be implemented in linear time—do you see how to do it?

TopoSort

Input: directed acyclic graph $G = (V, E)$ in adjacency-list representation.
Postcondition: the f-values of vertices constitute a topological ordering of G.

---

mark all vertices as unexplored
$curLabel := |V|$ // keeps track of ordering
for every $v \in V$ **do**
    if v is unexplored **then**   // in a prior DFS
        DFS-Topo (G, v)

Second, we must add a line of code to DFS that assigns an f-value to a vertex. The right time to do this is immediately upon completion of the DFS call initiated at v.

DFS-Topo

Input: graph $G = (V, E)$ in adjacency-list representation, and a vertex $s \in V$.
Postcondition: every vertex reachable from s is marked as "explored" and has an assigned f-value.

---

mark s as explored
for each edge (s, v) in s's outgoing adjacency list **do**
    if v is unexplored **then**
        DFS-Topo (G, v)
$f(s) := curLabel$ // s's position in ordering
$curLabel := curLabel - 1$ // work right-to-left

8.5.5 An Example

Suppose the input graph is the graph in Quiz 8.3. The TopoSort algorithm initializes the global variable $curLabel$ to the number of vertices, which is 4. The outer loop in TopoSort iterates through the vertices in an arbitrary order; let's assume this order is v, t, s, w. In the first iteration, because v is not marked as explored, the algorithm invokes the DFS-Topo subroutine with starting vertex v. The only outgoing edge from v is (v, t), and the next step is to recursively call DFS-Topo with starting vertex t. This call returns immediately (as t has no outgoing edges), at which point $f(t)$ is set to 4 and *curLabel* is decremented from 4 to 3. Next, the DFS-Topo call at v completes (as v has no other outgoing edges), at which point $f(v)$ is set to 3 and *curLabel* is decremented from 3 to 2. At this point, the TopoSort algorithm resumes its linear scan of the vertices in its outer loop. The next vertex is t; because t has already been marked as explored in the first call to DFS-Topo, the TopoSort algorithm skips it. Because the next vertex (which is s) has not yet been explored, the algorithm invokes DFS-Topo from s. From s, DFS-Topo skips v (which is already marked as explored) and recursively calls DFS-Topo at the newly discovered vertex w. The call at w completes immediately (the only outgoing edge is to the previously explored vertex t), at which point $f(w)$ is set to 2 and *curLabel* is decremented from 2 to 1. Finally, the DFS-Topo call at vertex s completes, and $f(s)$ is set to 1. The resulting topological ordering is the same as that in Figure 8.10(b).

Quiz 8.4

What happens when the TopoSort algorithm is run on a graph with a directed cycle?

a) The algorithm might or might not loop forever.

b) The algorithm always loops forever.

c) The algorithm always halts, and may or may not successfully compute a topological ordering.

d) The algorithm always halts, and never successfully computes a topological ordering.

(See Section 8.5.7 for the solution and discussion.)

8.5.6   Correctness and Running Time

The TopoSort algorithm correctly computes a topological ordering of a directed acyclic graph, and does so in linear time.

Theorem 8.8 (Properties of TopoSort) *For   every   directed acyclic graph $G = (V, E)$ in adjacency-list representation:*

(a) *At the conclusion of* TopoSort, *every vertex v has been assigned an f-value, and these f-values constitute a topological ordering of G.*

(b) *The running time of* TopoSort *is $O(m+n)$, where $m = |E|$ and $n = |V|$.*

Proof: The TopoSort algorithm runs in linear time for the usual reasons. It explores each edge only once (from its tail), and therefore performs only a constant number of operations for each vertex or edge. This implies an overall running time of $O(m + n)$.

For correctness, first note that DFS-Topo will be called from each vertex $v \in V$ exactly once, when v is encountered for the first time, and that v is assigned a label when this call completes. Thus, every vertex receives a label, and by decrementing the *curLabel* variable with every label assignment, the algorithm ensures that each vertex v gets a distinct label $f(v)$ from the set $\{1, 2, \ldots, |V|\}$. To see why these labels constitute a topological ordering, consider an arbitrary edge (v, w); we must argue that $f(v) < f(w)$. There are two cases, depending on which of v, w the algorithm discovers first.[33]

If v is discovered before w, then DFS-Topo is invoked with starting vertex v before w has been marked as explored. As w is reachable from v (via the edge (v, w)), this call to DFS-Topo eventually discovers w and recursively calls DFS-Topo at w. By the last-in first-out nature of recursive calls, the call to DFS-Topo at w completes before that at v. Because labels are assigned in decreasing order, w is assigned a larger f-value than v, as required.

Second, suppose w is discovered by the TopoSort algorithm before v. Because G is a directed acyclic graph, there is no path from w back to v; otherwise, combining such a path with the edge (v, w) would produce a directed cycle (Figure 8.13). Thus, the call to DFS-Topo starting at w cannot discover v and completes with v still unexplored. Once again, the DFS-Topo call at w completes before that at v and hence $f(v) < f(w)$. *QED*

---

[33]Both cases are possible, as we saw in Section 8.5.5.

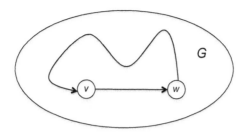

Figure 8.13: A directed acyclic graph cannot contain both an edge (v, w) and a path from w back to v.

8.5.7   Solution to Quizzes 8.3–8.4

Solution to Quiz 8.3

Correct answer: (c). Figure 8.14 shows two different topological orderings of the graph—you should check that these are the only ones.

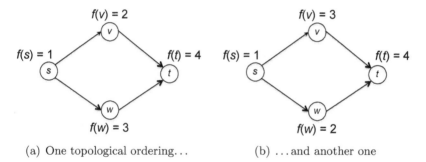

(a) One topological ordering...   (b) ...and another one

Figure 8.14: Two topological orderings of the graph in Quiz 8.3.

Solution to Quiz 8.4

Correct answer: (d). The algorithm always halts: There are only $|V|$ iterations of the outer loop, and each iteration either does nothing or invokes depth-first search (with minor additional bookkeeping). Depth-first search always halts, whether or not the input graph is directed acyclic (Theorem 8.5), and so `TopoSort` does as well. Any chance it halts with a topological ordering? No way—it is impossible to topologically sort the vertices of any graph with a directed cycle (recall Section 8.5.2).

*8.6   Computing Strongly Connected Components

Next we'll learn an even more interesting application of depth-first search: computing the strongly connected components of a directed graph.[34] Our algorithm will be just as blazingly fast as in the undirected case (Section 8.3), although less straightforward. Computing strongly connected components is a more challenging problem than topological sorting, and one pass of depth-first search won't be enough. So, we'll use two![35]

8.6.1   Defining Strongly Connected Components

What do we even mean by a "connected component" of a directed graph? For example, how many connected components does the graph in Figure 8.15 have?

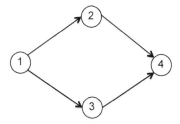

Figure 8.15: How many connected components?

It's tempting to say that this graph has one connected component—if it were a physical object, with the edges corresponding to strings tying the vertices together, we could pick it up and it would hang together in one piece. But remember how we defined connected components in the undirected case (Section 8.3), as maximal regions within which you can get from anywhere to anywhere else. There is no way to "move to the left" in the graph in Figure 8.15, so it's not the case that you can get from anywhere to anywhere else.

---

[34]Starred sections like this one are the more difficult sections; they can be skipped on a first reading.

[35]Actually, there *is* a somewhat tricky way to compute the strongly connected components of a directed graph with only one pass of depth-first search; see the paper "Depth-First Search and Linear Graph Algorithms," by Robert E. Tarjan (*SIAM Journal on Computing*, 1973).

A *strongly connected component* or *SCC* of a directed graph is a maximal subset $S \subseteq V$ of vertices such that there is a directed path from any vertex in S to any other vertex in S.[36] For example, the strongly connected components of the graph in Figure 8.16 are $\{1, 3, 5\}$, $\{11\}$, $\{2, 4, 7, 9\}$, and $\{6, 8, 10\}$. Within each component, it's possible to get from anywhere to anywhere else (as you should check). Each component is maximal subject to this property, as there's no way to "move to the left" from one SCC to another.

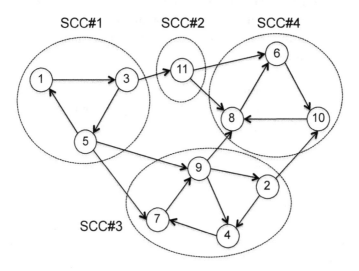

Figure 8.16: A graph with vertex set $\{1, 2, 3, \ldots, 11\}$ and four strongly connected components.

The relationships between the four SCCs of the graph in Figure 8.16 mirror those between the four vertices in the graph in Figure 8.15. More generally, if you squint, *every* directed graph can be viewed as a directed acyclic graph built up from its SCCs.

Proposition 8.9 (The SCC Meta-Graph Is Directed Acyclic)
Let $G = (V, E)$ be a directed graph. Define the corresponding meta-graph $H = (X, F)$ *with one meta-vertex $x \in X$ per SCC of G and a*

---

[36] As with connected components in undirected graphs (footnote 18), the strongly connected components of a directed graph G are precisely the equivalence classes of an equivalence relation $\sim_G$, where $v \sim_G w$ if and only if there are directed paths from v to w and from w to v in G. The proof that $\sim_G$ is an equivalence relation mirrors that in the undirected case (footnote 18).

meta-edge (x, y) *in* F *whenever there is an edge in* G *from a vertex in the SCC corresponding to* x *to one in the SCC corresponding to* y. *Then* H *is a directed acyclic graph.*

For example, the directed acyclic graph in Figure 8.15 is the meta-graph corresponding to the directed graph in Figure 8.16.

Proof of Proposition 8.9: If the meta-graph H had a directed cycle with $k \geq 2$ vertices, the corresponding cycle of allegedly distinct SCCs $S_1, S_2, \ldots, S_k$ in G would collapse to a single SCC: You can already travel freely within each of the S_i's, and the cycle then permits travel between any pair of the S_i's. $\mathcal{QED}$

Proposition 8.9 implies that every directed graph can be viewed at two levels of granularity. Zooming out, you focus only on the (acyclic) relationships among its SCCs; zooming in to a specific SCC reveals its fine-grained structure.

Quiz 8.5

Consider a directed acyclic graph with n vertices and m edges. What are the minimum and maximum number of strongly connected components that the graph could have, respectively?

a) 1 and 1

b) 1 and n

c) 1 and m

d) n and n

(See Section 8.6.7 for the solution and discussion.)

8.6.2 Why Depth-First Search?

To see why graph search might help in computing strongly connected components, let's return to the graph in Figure 8.16. Suppose we invoke depth-first search (or breadth-first search, for that matter) from the vertex 6. The algorithm will find everything reachable from 6 and nothing more, discovering $\{6, 8, 10\}$, which is exactly one of the strongly connected components. The bad case is if we instead initiate a graph search from vertex 1, in which case all the vertices (not only $\{1, 3, 5\}$) are discovered and we learn nothing about the component structure.

The take-away is that graph search can uncover strongly connected components, provided you start from the right place. Intuitively, we want to first discover a "sink SCC," meaning an SCC with no outgoing edges (like SCC#4 in Figure 8.16), and then work backward. In terms of the meta-graph in Proposition 8.9, it seems we want to discover the SCCs in reverse topological order, plucking off sink SCCs one by one. We've already seen in Section 8.5 that topological orderings are right in the wheelhouse of depth-first search, and this is the reason why our algorithm will use two passes of depth-first search. The first pass computes a magical ordering in which to process the vertices, and the second follows this ordering to discover the SCCs one by one. This two-pass strategy is known as *Kosaraju's algorithm.*[37]

For shock value, here's an advance warning of what Kosaraju's algorithm looks like from 30,000 feet:

Kosaraju (**High-Level**)

1. Let G^{rev} denote the input graph G with the direction of every edge reversed.

2. Call DFS from every vertex of G^{rev}, processed in arbitrary order, to compute a position $f(v)$ for each vertex v.

3. Call DFS from every vertex of G, processed from highest to lowest position, to compute the identity of each vertex's strongly connected component.

You might have at least a little intuition for the second and third steps of Kosaraju's algorithm. The second step presumably does

---

[37]The algorithm first appeared in an unpublished paper by S. Rao Kosaraju in 1978. Micha Sharir also discovered the algorithm and published it in the paper "A Strong-Connectivity Algorithm and Its Applications in Data Flow Analysis" (*Computers & Mathematics with Applications*, 1981). The algorithm is also sometimes called the Kosaraju-Sharir algorithm.

something similar to the `TopoSort` algorithm from Section 8.5, with
the goal of processing the SCCs of the input graph in the third step in
reverse topological order. (Caveat: We thought about the `TopoSort`
algorithm only in DAGs, and here we have a general directed graph.)
The third step is hopefully analogous to the `UCC` algorithm from
Section 8.3 for undirected graphs. (Caveat: In undirected graphs, the
order in which you process the vertices doesn't matter; in directed
graphs, as we've seen, it does.) But what's up with the first step?
Why does the first pass work with the reversal of the input graph?

8.6.3   Why the Reversed Graph?

Let's first explore the more natural idea of invoking the `TopoSort`
algorithm from Section 8.5 on the original input graph $G = (V, E)$.
Recall that this algorithm has an outer for loop that makes a pass
over the vertices of G in an arbitrary order; initiates depth-first
search whenever it encounters a not-yet-explored vertex; and assigns
a position $f(v)$ to a vertex v when the depth-first search initiated at v
completes. The positions are assigned in decreasing order, from $|V|$
down to 1.

The `TopoSort` algorithm was originally motivated by the case of
a directed acyclic input graph, but it can be used to compute vertex
positions for an arbitrary directed graph (Quiz 8.4). We're hoping
these vertex positions are somehow helpful for quickly identifying a
good starting vertex for our second depth-first search pass, ideally a
vertex in a sink SCC of G, with no outgoing edges. There's reason
for optimism: With a directed acyclic graph G, the vertex positions
constitute a topological ordering (Theorem 8.8), and the vertex in
the last position must be a sink vertex of G, with no outgoing edges.
(Any such edges would travel backward in the ordering.) Perhaps
with a general directed graph G, the vertex in the last position always
belongs to a sink SCC?

An Example

Sadly, no. For example, suppose we run the `TopoSort` algorithm on
the graph in Figure 8.16. Suppose that we process the vertices in
increasing order, with vertex 1 considered first. (In this case, all
the vertices are discovered in the first iteration of the outer loop.)

Suppose further that depth-first search traverses edge $(3, 5)$ before $(3, 11)$, $(5, 7)$ before $(5, 9)$, $(9, 4)$ before $(9, 2)$, and $(9, 2)$ before $(9, 8)$. In this case, you should check that the vertex positions wind up being:

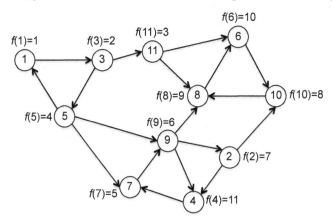

Against our wishes, the vertex in the last position (vertex 4) does not belong to the sink SCC. The one piece of good news is that the vertex in the *first* position (vertex 1) belongs to a source SCC (meaning an SCC with no incoming edges).

What if we instead process the vertices in descending order? If depth-first search traverses edge $(11, 6)$ before $(11, 8)$ and edge $(9, 2)$ before $(9, 4)$, then (as you should check) the vertex positions are:

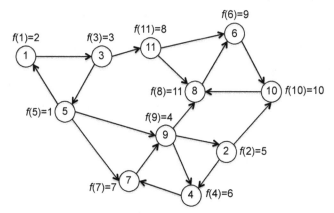

This time, the vertex in the last position is in the sink SCC, but we know this doesn't happen in general. More intriguingly, the vertex in the first position belongs to the source SCC, albeit a different vertex from this SCC than last time. Could this be true in general?

The First Vertex Resides in a Source SCC

In fact, something stronger is true: If we label each SCC of G with the smallest position of one of its vertices, these labels constitute a topological ordering of the meta-graph of SCCs defined in Proposition 8.9.

Theorem 8.10 (Topological Ordering of the SCCs) *Let G be a directed graph, with the vertices ordered arbitrarily, and for each vertex $v \in V$ let $f(v)$ denote the position of v computed by the TopoSort algorithm. Let S_1, S_2 denote two SCCs of G, and suppose G has an edge (v, w) with $v \in S_1$ and $w \in S_2$. Then,*

$$\min_{x \in S_1} f(x) < \min_{y \in S_2} f(y).$$

Proof: The proof is similar to the correctness of the TopoSort algorithm (Theorem 8.8, which is worth re-reading now). Let S_1, S_2 denote two SCCs of G, and consider two cases.[38] First, suppose that the TopoSort algorithm discovers and initiates depth-first search from a vertex s of S_1 before any vertex of S_2. Because there is an edge from a vertex v in S_1 to a vertex w in S_2 and S_1 and S_2 are SCCs, every vertex of S_2 is reachable from s—to reach some vertex $y \in S_2$, paste together a $s \rightsquigarrow v$ path within S_1, the edge (v, w), and a $w \rightsquigarrow y$ path within S_2. By the last-in first-out nature of recursive calls, the depth-first search initiated at s will not complete until after all the vertices of S_2 have been fully explored. Because vertex positions are assigned in decreasing order, v's position will be smaller than that of every vertex of S_2.

For the second case, suppose the TopoSort algorithm discovers a vertex $s \in S_2$ before any vertex of S_1. Because G's meta-graph is directed acyclic (Proposition 8.9), there is no directed path from s to any vertex of S_1. (Such a path would collapse S_1 and S_2 into a single SCC.) Thus, the depth-first search initiated at s completes after discovering all the vertices of S_2 (and possibly other stuff) and none of the vertices of S_1. In this case, *every* vertex of S_1 is assigned a position smaller than that of every vertex of S_2. $\mathcal{QED}$

Theorem 8.10 implies that the vertex in the first position always resides in a source SCC, just as we hoped. For consider the vertex v

---

[38]Both cases are possible, as we saw in the preceding example.

with $f(v) = 1$, inhabiting the SCC S. If S were not a source SCC, with an incoming edge from a different SCC S', then by Theorem 8.10 the smallest vertex position in S' would be less than 1, which is impossible.

Summarizing, after one pass of depth-first search, we can immediately identify a vertex in a source SCC. The only problem? We want to identify a vertex in a *sink* SCC. The fix? *Reverse the graph first.*

Reversing the Graph

Quiz 8.6

Let G be a directed graph and G^{rev} a copy of G with the direction of every edge reversed. How are the SCCs of G and G^{rev} related? (Choose all that apply.)

a) In general, they are unrelated.

b) Every SCC of G is also an SCC of G^{rev}, and conversely.

c) Every source SCC of G is also a source SCC of G^{rev}.

d) Every sink SCC of G becomes a source SCC of G^{rev}.

(See Section 8.6.7 for the solution and discussion.)

The following corollary rewrites Theorem 8.10 for the reversed graph, using the solution to Quiz 8.6.

Corollary 8.11 *Let G be a directed graph, with the vertices ordered arbitrarily, and for each vertex $v \in V$ let $f(v)$ denote the position of v computed by the* TopoSort *algorithm on the reversed graph G^{rev}. Let S_1, S_2 denote two SCCs of G, and suppose G has an edge (v, w) with $v \in S_1$ and $w \in S_2$. Then,*

$$\min_{x \in S_1} f(x) > \min_{y \in S_2} f(y). \tag{8.1}$$

In particular, the vertex in the first position resides in a sink SCC of G, and is the perfect starting point for a second depth-first search pass.

8.6.4   Pseudocode for Kosaraju

We now have all our ducks in a row: We run one pass of depth-first search (via TopoSort) on the reversed graph, which computes a magical ordering in which to visit the vertices, and a second pass (via the DFS-Topo subroutine) to discover the SCCs in reverse topological order, peeling them off one by one like the layers of an onion.

Kosaraju

Input: directed graph $G = (V, E)$ in adjacency-list representation, with $V = \{1, 2, 3, \ldots, n\}$.
Postcondition: for every $v, w \in V$, $scc(v) = scc(w)$ if and only if v, w are in the same SCC of G.

$G^{rev} := G$ with all edges reversed
mark all vertices of G^{rev} as unexplored

```
// first pass of depth-first search
// (computes f(v)'s, the magical ordering)
TopoSort (G^rev)

// second pass of depth-first search
// (finds SCCs in reverse topological order)
mark all vertices of G as unexplored
numSCC := 0                    // global variable
for each v ∈ V, in increasing order of f(v) do
    if v is unexplored then
        numSCC := numSCC + 1
        // assign scc-values (details below)
        DFS-SCC (G, v)
```

Three implementation details:[39]

1. The most obvious way to implement the algorithm is to literally make a second copy of the input graph, with all edges reversed, and feed it to the TopoSort subroutine. A smarter implementation runs the TopoSort algorithm *backward* in the original input

---

[39] To really appreciate these, it's best to implement the algorithm yourself (see Programming Problem 8.10).

graph, by replacing the clause "each edge (s, v) in s's outgoing adjacency list" in the DFS-Topo subroutine of Section 8.5 with "each edge (v, s) in s's incoming adjacency list."

2. For best results, the first pass of depth-first search should export an array that contains the vertices (or pointers to them) in order of their positions, so that the second pass can process them with a simple array scan. This adds only constant overhead to the TopoSort subroutine (as you should check).

3. The DFS-SCC subroutine is the same as DFS, with one additional line of bookkeeping:

DFS-SCC

Input: directed graph $G = (V, E)$ in adjacency-list representation, and a vertex $s \in V$.
Postcondition: every vertex reachable from s is marked as "explored" and has an assigned *scc*-value.

---

mark s as explored
$scc(s) := numSCC$ // global variable above
for each edge (s, v) in s's outgoing adjacency list **do**
    if v is unexplored **then**
        DFS-SCC (G, v)

8.6.5   An Example

Let's verify on our running example that we get what we want—that the second pass of depth-first search discovers the SCCs in reverse topological order. Suppose the graph in Figure 8.16 is the reversal G^{rev} of the input graph. We computed in Section 8.6.3 two ways in which the TopoSort algorithm might assign f-values to the vertices of this graph; let's use the first one. Here's the (unreversed) input graph with its vertices annotated with these vertex positions:

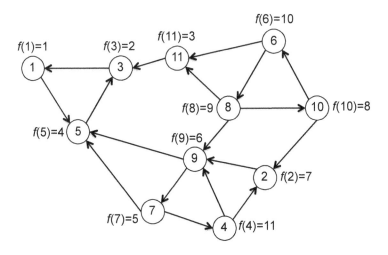

The second pass iterates through the vertices in increasing order of vertex position. Thus, the first call to DFS-SCC is initiated at the vertex in the first position (which happens to be vertex 1); it discovers the vertices 1, 3, and 5 and marks them as the vertices of the first SCC. The algorithm proceeds to consider the vertex in the second position (vertex 3); it was already explored by the first call to DFS-SCC and is skipped. The vertex in the third position (vertex 11) has not yet been discovered and is the next starting point for DFS-SCC. The only outgoing edge of this vertex travels to an already-explored vertex (vertex 3), so 11 is the only member of the second SCC. The algorithm skips the vertex in the fourth position (vertex 5, already explored) and next initiates DFS-SCC from vertex 7, the vertex in the fifth position. This search discovers the vertices 2, 4, 7, and 9 (the other outgoing edges are to the already-explored vertex 5) and classifies them as the third SCC. The algorithm skips vertex 9 and then vertex 2, and finally invokes DFS-SCC from vertex 10 to discover the final SCC (comprising the vertices 6, 8, and 10).

8.6.6   Correctness and Running Time

The Kosaraju algorithm is correct and blazingly fast for every directed graph, not merely for our running example.

Theorem 8.12 (Properties of Kosaraju) *For   every   directed graph $G = (V, E)$ in adjacency-list representation:*

(a) At the conclusion of Kosaraju, for every pair v, w of vertices, $scc(v) = scc(w)$ if and only if v and w belong to the same strongly connected component of G.

(b) The running time of Kosaraju is $O(m+n)$, where $m = |E|$ and $n = |V|$.

We've already discussed all the ingredients needed for the proof. The algorithm can be implemented in $O(m + n)$ time, with a small hidden constant factor, for the usual reasons. Each of the two passes of depth-first search does a constant number of operations per vertex or edge, and the extra bookkeeping increases the running time by only a constant factor.

The algorithm also correctly computes all the SCCs: Each time it initiates a new call to DFS-SCC, the algorithm discovers exactly one new SCC, which is a sink SCC relative to the graph of not-yet-explored vertices (that is, an SCC in which all outgoing edges lead to already-explored vertices).[40]

8.6.7   Solutions to Quizzes 8.5–8.6

Solution to Quiz 8.5

Correct answer: (d). In a directed acyclic graph $G = (V, E)$, every vertex is in its own strongly connected component (for a total of $n = |V|$ SCCs). To see this, fix a topological ordering of G (Section 8.5.1), with each vertex $v \in V$ assigned a distinct label $f(v)$. (One exists, by Theorem 8.6.) Edges of G travel only from smaller to larger f-values, so for every pair $v, w \in V$ of vertices, there is either no $v \rightsquigarrow w$ path (if $f(v) > f(w)$) or no $w \rightsquigarrow v$ path (if $f(w) > f(v)$) in G. This precludes two vertices from inhabiting the same SCC.

---

[40]For a more formal proof, consider a call to the DFS-SCC subroutine with a starting vertex v that belongs to an SCC S. Corollary 8.11 implies that directed paths out of v can reach only SCCs containing at least one vertex assigned a position earlier than v's. Because the Kosaraju algorithm processes vertices in order of position, all the vertices in SCCs reachable from v have already been explored by the algorithm. (Remember that once the algorithm finds one vertex from an SCC, it finds them all.) Thus, the edges going out of S reach only already-explored vertices. This call to DFS-SCC discovers the vertices of S and nothing more, as there are no available avenues for it to trespass on other SCCs. As every call to DFS-SCC discovers a single SCC and every vertex is eventually considered, the Kosaraju algorithm correctly identifies all the SCCs.

Solution to Quiz 8.6

Correct answers: (b),(d). Two vertices v, w of a directed graph are in the same strongly connected component if and only if there is both a directed path P_1 from v to w and a directed path P_2 from w to v. This property holds for v and w in G if and only if it holds in G^{rev}—in the latter, using the reversed version of P_1 to get from w to v and the reversed version of P_2 to get from v to w. We can conclude that the SCCs of G and G^{rev} are exactly the same. Source SCCs of G (with no incoming edges) become sink SCCs of G^{rev} (with no outgoing edges), and sink SCCs become source SCCs. More generally, there is an edge from a vertex in SCC S_1 to a vertex SCC S_2 in G if and only if there is a corresponding edge from a vertex in S_2 to a vertex in S_1 in G^{rev} (Figure 8.17).[41]

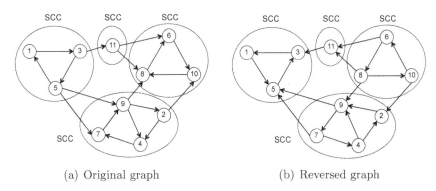

(a) Original graph   (b) Reversed graph

Figure 8.17: A graph and its reversal have the same strongly connected components.

8.7   The Structure of the Web

You now know a collection of for-free graph primitives. If you have graph data, you can apply these blazingly fast algorithms even if you're not sure how you'll use the results. For example, with a directed graph, why not compute its strongly connected components to get a sense of what it looks like? Next, we explore this idea in a huge and hugely interesting directed graph, the *Web graph*.

---

[41]In other words, the meta-graph of G^{rev} (Proposition 8.9) is simply the meta-graph of G with every edge reversed.

8.7.1   The Web Graph

In the Web graph, vertices correspond to Web pages, and edges to hyperlinks. This graph is directed, with an edge pointing from the page that contains the link to the landing page for the link. For example, my home page corresponds to a vertex in this graph, with outgoing edges corresponding to links to pages that list my books, my courses, and so on. There are also incoming edges corresponding to links to my home page, perhaps from my co-authors or lists of instructors of online courses (Figure 8.18).

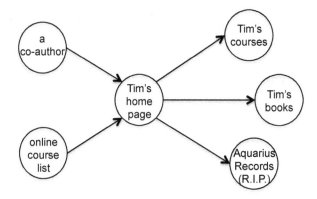

Figure 8.18: A minuscule piece of the Web graph.

While the Web's origins date back to roughly 1990, the Web really started to explode about five years later. By 2000 (still the Stone Age in Internet years), the Web graph was already so big as to defy imagination, and researchers were keenly interested in understanding its structure.[42] This section describes a famous study from that time that explored the structure of the Web graph by computing its strongly connected components.[43] The graph had more than 200

---

[42]Constructing this graph requires crawling (a big chunk of) the Web by repeatedly following hyperlinks, and this is a significant engineering feat in its own right.

[43]This study is described in the very readable paper "Graph Structure in the Web," by Andrei Broder, Ravi Kumar, Farzin Maghoul, Prabhakar Raghavan, Sridhar Rajagopalan, Raymie Stata, Andrew Tomkins, and Janet Wiener (*Computer Networks*, 2000). Google barely existed at this time, and the study used data from Web crawls by the search engine Alta Vista (which is now long since defunct).

million vertices and 1.5 billion edges, so linear-time algorithms were absolutely essential![44]

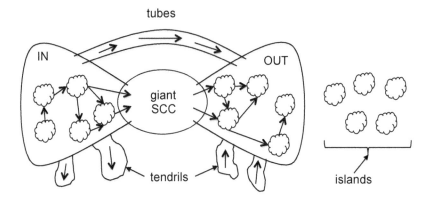

Figure 8.19: Visualizing the Web graph as a "bow tie." Roughly the same number of Web pages belong to the giant SCC, to IN, to OUT, and to the rest of the graph.

8.7.2   The Bow Tie

The Broder et al. study computed the strongly connected components of the Web graph, and explained its findings using the "bow tie" depicted in Figure 8.19. The knot of the bow tie is the biggest strongly connected component of the graph, comprising roughly 28% of its vertices. The title "giant" is well earned by this SCC, as the next-largest SCC was over two orders of magnitude smaller.[45] The giant SCC can be interpreted as the core of the Web, with every page reachable from every other page by a sequence of hyperlinks.

The smaller SCCs can be placed into a few categories. From some, it's possible to reach the giant SCC (but not vice versa); this is the left ("IN") part of the bow tie. For example, a newly created Web page with a link to some page in the giant SCC would appear in this part. Symmetrically, the "OUT" part is all the SCCs reachable from the

---

[44]The study pre-dates modern massive data processing frameworks like MapReduce and Hadoop, and this was an intimidating input size at the time.

[45]Remember that all it takes to collapse two SCCs into one is one edge in each direction. Intuitively, it would be pretty weird if there were two massive SCCs, with no edge going between them in at least one direction.

giant SCC, but not vice versa. One example of an SCC in this part is a corporate Web site for which the company policy dictates that all hyperlinks from its pages stay within the site. There's also some other weird stuff: "tubes," which travel from IN to OUT, bypassing the giant SCC; "tendrils," which are reachable from IN or which can reach OUT (but not belonging to the giant SCC); and "islands" of Web pages that cannot reach or be reached from almost any other part of the Web.

8.7.3   Main Findings

Perhaps the most surprising finding of the study is that the giant SCC, the IN part, the OUT part, and the weird stuff all have roughly the same size (with $\approx$ 24–28% of the vertices each). Before this study, many people expected the giant SCC to be much bigger than just 28% of the Web. A second interesting finding is that the giant SCC is internally richly connected: it has roughly 56 million Web pages, but you typically need to follow fewer than 20 hyperlinks to get from one to another.[46] The rest of the Web graph is more poorly connected, with long paths often necessary to get from one vertex to another.

You'd be right to wonder whether any of these findings are an artifact of the now prehistoric snapshot of the Web graph that the experiment used. While the exact numbers have changed over time as the Web graph has grown and evolved, more recent follow-up studies re-evaluating the structure of the Web graph suggest that Broder et al.'s qualitative findings remain accurate.[47]

The Upshot

★ Breadth-first search (BFS) explores a graph

---

[46]The presence of ubiquitous short paths is also known as the "small world property," which is closely related to the popular phrase "six degrees of separation."

[47]There continues to be lots of cool research about the Web graph and other information networks; for example, about how the Web graph evolves over time, on the dynamics of how information spreads through such a graph, and on how to identify "communities" or other meaningful fine-grained structure. Blazingly fast graph primitives play a crucial role in much of this research. For an introduction to these topics, check out the textbook *Networks, Crowds, and Markets: Reasoning About a Highly Connected World*, by David Easley and Jon Kleinberg (Cambridge University Press, 2010).

cautiously, in layers.

☆ BFS can be implemented in linear time using a queue data structure.

☆ BFS can be used to compute the lengths of shortest paths between a starting vertex and all other vertices in linear time.

☆ A connected component of an undirected graph is a maximal subset of vertices such that there is a path between each pair of its vertices.

☆ An efficient graph search algorithm like BFS can be used to compute the connected components of an undirected graph in linear time.

☆ Depth-first search (DFS) explores a graph aggressively, backtracking only when necessary.

☆ DFS can be implemented in linear time using a stack data structure (or recursion).

☆ A topological ordering of a directed graph assigns distinct numbers to the vertices, with every edge traveling from a smaller number to a bigger one.

☆ A directed graph has a topological ordering if and only if it is a directed acyclic graph.

☆ DFS can be used to compute a topological ordering of a directed acyclic graph in linear time.

☆ A strongly connected component of a directed graph is a maximal subset of vertices such that there is a directed path from any vertex in the set to any other vertex in the set.

☆ DFS can be used to compute the strongly connected components of a directed graph in linear time.

> ✰ In the Web graph, a giant strongly connected
> component contains roughly 28% of the vertices
> and is internally richly connected.

Test Your Understanding

Problem 8.1 *(S)* Which of the following statements hold? As usual, n and m denote the number of vertices and edges, respectively, of a graph. (Choose all that apply.)

a) Breadth-first search can be used to compute the connected components of an undirected graph in $O(m + n)$ time.

b) Breadth-first search can be used to compute the lengths of shortest paths from a starting vertex to every other vertex in $O(m+n)$ time, where "shortest" means having the fewest number of edges.

c) Depth-first search can be used to compute the strongly connected components of a directed graph in $O(m + n)$ time.

d) Depth-first search can be used to compute a topological ordering of a directed acyclic graph in $O(m + n)$ time.

Problem 8.2 *(S)* What is the running time of depth-first search, as a function of n and m (the number of vertices and edges), if the input graph is represented by an adjacency matrix (and NOT adjacency lists)? You may assume the graph does not have parallel edges.

a) $\Theta(m + n)$

b) $\Theta(m + n \log n)$

c) $\Theta(n^2)$

d) $\Theta(m \cdot n)$

Problem 8.3 This problem explores the relationship between two definitions concerning graph distances. In this problem, we consider only graphs that are undirected and connected. The *diameter* of a graph is the maximum, over all choices of vertices v and w, of the shortest-path distance between v and w.[48] Next, for a vertex v, let $l(v)$ denote the maximum, over all vertices w, of the shortest-path distance between v and w. The *radius* of a graph is the minimum value of $l(v)$, over all choices of the vertex v.

Which of the following inequalities relating the radius r to the diameter d hold in every undirected connected graph? (Choose all that apply.)

a) $r \leq \frac{d}{2}$

b) $r \leq d$

c) $r \geq \frac{d}{2}$

d) $r \geq d$

Problem 8.4 When does a directed graph have a unique topological ordering?

a) Whenever it is directed acyclic.

b) Whenever it has a unique cycle.

c) Whenever it contains a directed path that visits every vertex exactly once.

d) None of the other options are correct.

Problem 8.5 Consider running the `TopoSort` algorithm (Section 8.5) on a directed graph G that is not directed acyclic. The algorithm will not compute a topological ordering (as none exist). Does it compute an ordering that minimizes the number of edges that travel backward (Figure 8.20)? (Choose all that apply.)

a) The `TopoSort` algorithm always computes an ordering of the vertices that minimizes the number of backward edges.

b) The `TopoSort` algorithm never computes an ordering of the vertices that minimizes the number of backward edges.

---

[48]Recall that the shortest-path distance between v and w is the fewest number of edges in a v-w path.

c) There are examples in which the `TopoSort` algorithm computes an ordering of the vertices that minimizes the number of backward edges, and also examples in which it doesn't.

d) The `TopoSort` algorithm computes an ordering of the vertices that minimizes the number of backward edges if and only if the input graph is a directed cycle.

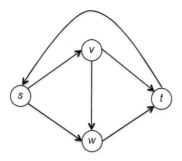

Figure 8.20: A graph with no topological ordering. In the ordering s, v, w, t, the only backward edge is (t, s).

Problem 8.6 If you add one new edge to a directed graph G, then the number of strongly connected components... (Choose all that apply.)

a) ...might or might not remain the same (depending on G and the new edge).

b) ...cannot decrease.

c) ...cannot increase.

d) ...cannot decrease by more than 1.

Problem 8.7 *(S)* Recall the `Kosaraju` algorithm from Section 8.6, which uses two passes of depth-first search to compute the strongly connected components of a directed graph. Which of the following statements are true? (Choose all that apply.)

a) The algorithm would remain correct if it used breadth-first search instead of depth-first search in both its passes.

b) The algorithm would remain correct if we used breadth-first search instead of depth-first search in its first pass.

c) The algorithm would remain correct if we used breadth-first search instead of depth-first search in its second pass.

d) The algorithm is not correct unless it uses depth-first search in both its passes.

Problem 8.8 *(S)* Recall that in the `Kosaraju` algorithm, the first pass of depth-first search operates on the reversed version of the input graph and the second on the original input graph. Which of the following statements are true? (Choose all that apply.)

a) The algorithm would remain correct if in the first pass it assigned vertex positions in increasing (rather than decreasing) order and in the second pass considered the vertices in decreasing (rather than increasing) order of vertex position.

b) The algorithm would remain correct if it used the original input graph in its first pass and the reversed graph in its second pass.

c) The algorithm would remain correct if it used the original input graph in both passes, provided in the first pass it assigned vertex positions in increasing (rather than decreasing) order.

d) The algorithm would remain correct if it used the original input graph in both passes, provided in the second pass it considered the vertices in decreasing (rather than increasing) order of vertex position.

Challenge Problems

Problem 8.9 In the *2SAT* problem, you are given a set of clauses, each of which is the disjunction (logical "or") of two literals. (A literal is a Boolean variable or the negation of a Boolean variable.) You would like to assign a value "true" or "false" to each of the variables so that all the clauses are satisfied, with at least one true literal in each clause. For example, if the input contains the three clauses $x_1 \vee x_2$, $\neg x_1 \vee x_3$, and $\neg x_2 \vee \neg x_3$, then one way to satisfy all of them is to set x_1 and x_3 to "true" and x_2 to "false."[49] Of the seven other possible truth assignments, only one satisfies all three clauses.

Design an algorithm that determines whether or not a given 2SAT instance has at least one satisfying assignment. (Your algorithm is responsible only for deciding whether or not a satisfying assignment exists; it need not exhibit such an assignment.) Your algorithm should run in $O(m + n)$ time, where m and n are the number of clauses and variables, respectively.

[Hint: Show how to solve the problem by computing the strongly connected components of a suitably defined directed graph.]

Programming Problems

Problem 8.10 Implement in your favorite programming language the Kosaraju algorithm from Section 8.6, and use it to compute the sizes of the five biggest strongly connected components of different directed graphs. You can implement the iterative version of depth-first search, the recursive version (though see footnote 24), or both. (See www.algorithmsilluminated.org for test cases and challenge data sets.)

---

[49]The symbol "∨" stands for the logical "or" operation, while "¬" denotes the negation of a Boolean variable.

Chapter 9

Dijkstra's Shortest-Path Algorithm

We've arrived at another one of computer science's greatest hits: Dijkstra's shortest-path algorithm.[1] This algorithm works in any directed graph with nonnegative edge lengths, and it computes the lengths of shortest paths from a starting vertex to all other vertices. After formally defining the problem (Section 9.1), we describe the algorithm (Section 9.2), its proof of correctness (Section 9.3), and a straightforward implementation (Section 9.4). In the next chapter, we'll see a blazingly fast implementation of the algorithm that takes advantage of the heap data structure.

9.1 The Single-Source Shortest Path Problem

9.1.1 Problem Definition

Dijkstra's algorithm solves the *single-source shortest path problem*.[2]

Problem: Single-Source Shortest Paths

Input: A directed graph $G = (V, E)$, a starting vertex $s \in V$, and a nonnegative *length* ℓ_e for each edge $e \in E$.

Output: $dist(s, v)$ for every vertex $v \in V$.

---

[1]Discovered by Edsger W. Dijkstra in 1956 ("in about twenty minutes," he said in an interview many years later). Several other researchers independently discovered similar algorithms in the late 1950s.

[2]The term "source" in the name of the problem refers to the given starting vertex. We've already used the term "source vertex" to mean a vertex of a directed graph with no incoming edges (Section 8.5.2). To stay consistent with our terminology in Chapter 8, we'll stick with "starting vertex."

Recall that the notation $dist(s, v)$ denotes the length of a shortest path from s to v. (If there is no path at all from s to v, then $dist(s, v)$ is $+\infty$.) By the *length* of a path, we mean the sum of the lengths of its edges. For instance, in a graph in which every edge has length 1, the length of a path is just the number of edges in it. A *shortest* path from a vertex v to a vertex w is one with minimum length (among all v-w paths).

For example, if the graph represents a road network and the length of each edge represents the expected travel time from one end to the other, the single-source shortest path problem is the problem of computing driving times from an origin (the starting vertex) to all possible destinations.

Quiz 9.1

Consider the following input to the single-source shortest path problem, with starting vertex s and with each edge labeled with its length:

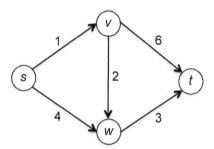

What are the shortest-path distances to s, v, w, and t, respectively?

a) $0, 1, 2, 3$

b) $0, 1, 3, 6$

c) $0, 1, 4, 6$

d) $0, 1, 4, 7$

(See Section 9.1.4 for the solution and discussion.)

9.1.2   Some Assumptions

For concreteness, we assume throughout this chapter that the input graph is directed. Dijkstra's algorithm applies equally well to undirected graphs after small cosmetic changes (as you should check). Our other assumption is significant. The problem statement already spells it out: We assume that the length of every edge is nonnegative. In many applications, like computing driving directions, edge lengths are automatically nonnegative (barring a time machine) and there's nothing to worry about. But remember that paths in a graph can represent abstract sequences of decisions. For example, perhaps you want to compute a profitable sequence of financial transactions that involves both buying and selling. This problem corresponds to finding a shortest path in a graph with edge lengths that are both positive and negative. You should *not* use Dijkstra's algorithm in applications with negative edge lengths; see also Section 9.3.1.[3]

9.1.3   Why Not Breadth-First Search?

We saw in Section 8.2 that one of the killer applications of breadth-first search is computing shortest-path distances from a starting vertex. Why do we need another shortest-path algorithm?

Remember that breadth-first search computes the minimum number of *edges* in a path from the starting vertex to every other vertex. This is the special case of the single-source shortest path problem in which every edge has length 1. We saw in Quiz 9.1 that, with general nonnegative edge lengths, a shortest path need not be a path with the fewest number of edges. Many applications of shortest paths, such as computing driving directions or a sequence of financial transactions, inevitably involve edges with different lengths.

But wait, you say; is the general problem really so different from this special case? Can't we just think of an edge with a longer length ℓ as a path of ℓ edges that each have length 1?:

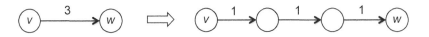

---

[3]In *Part 3* we'll learn about efficient algorithms for the more general single-source shortest path problem in which negative edge lengths are allowed, including the famous Bellman-Ford algorithm.

Indeed, there's no fundamental difference between an edge with a positive integral length ℓ and a path of ℓ length-1 edges. In principle, you can solve the single-source shortest path problem by expanding edges into paths of length-1 edges and applying breadth-first search to the expanded graph.

This is an example of a *reduction* from one problem to another—in this case, from the single-source shortest path problem with positive integer edge lengths to the special case of the problem in which every edge has length 1.

The major problem with this reduction is that it blows up the size of the graph. The blowup is not too bad if all the edge lengths are small integers, but this is not always the case in applications. The length of an edge could even be much bigger than the number of vertices and edges in the original graph! Breadth-first search would run in time linear in the size of the expanded graph, but this is not necessarily close to linear time in the size of the original graph. Dijkstra's algorithm can be viewed as a slick simulation of breadth-first search on the expanded graph, while working only with the original input graph and running in near-linear time.

On Reductions

A problem A *reduces* to a problem B if an algorithm that solves B can be easily translated into one that solves A. For example, the problem of computing the median element of an array reduces to the problem of sorting the array. Reductions are one of the most important concepts in the study of algorithms and their limitations, and they can also have great practical utility.

You should always be on the lookout for reductions. Whenever you encounter a seemingly new problem, always ask: Is the problem a disguised version of one you already know how to solve? Alternatively, can you reduce the general version of the problem to a special case?

9.1.4   Solution to Quiz 9.1

Correct answer: (b). No prizes for guessing that the shortest-path distance from s to itself is 0 and from s to v is 1. Vertex w is more interesting. One s-w path is the direct edge (s, w), which has length 4. But using more edges can decrease the total length: The path $s \to v \to w$ has length only $1 + 2 = 3$ and is the shortest s-w path. Similarly, each of the two-hop paths from s to t has length 7, while the zigzag path has length only $1 + 2 + 3 = 6$.

9.2   Dijkstra's Algorithm

9.2.1   Pseudocode

The high-level structure of Dijkstra's algorithm resembles that of our graph search algorithms.[4] Each iteration of its main loop processes one new vertex. The algorithm's sophistication lies in its clever rule for selecting which vertex to process next: the not-yet-processed vertex that appears to be closest to the starting vertex. The following elegant pseudocode makes this idea precise.

Dijkstra

Input: directed graph $G = (V, E)$ in adjacency-list representation, a vertex $s \in V$, a length $\ell_e \geq 0$ for each $e \in E$.
Postcondition: for every vertex v, the value $len(v)$ equals the true shortest-path distance $dist(s, v)$.

```
// Initialization
1  X := {s}
2  len(s) := 0, len(v) := +∞ for every v ≠ s
   // Main loop
3  while there is an edge (v, w) with v ∈ X, w ∉ X do
4      (v*, w*) := such an edge minimizing len(v) + ℓvw
5      add w* to X
6      len(w*) := len(v*) + ℓv*w*
```

---

[4]When all the edges have length 1, it's equivalent to breadth-first search (as you should check).

The set X contains the vertices that the algorithm has already dealt with. Initially, X contains only the starting vertex (and, of course, $len(s) = 0$), and the set grows like a mold until it covers all the vertices reachable from s. The algorithm assigns a finite value to the len-value of a vertex at the same time it adds the vertex to X. Each iteration of the main loop augments X by one new vertex, the head of some edge (v, w) crossing from X to $V - X$ (Figure 9.1). (If there is no such edge, the algorithm halts, with $len(v) = +\infty$ for all $v \notin X$.) There can be many such edges; the Dijkstra algorithm chooses one (v^*, w^*) that minimizes the *Dijkstra score*, which is defined as

$$len(v) + \ell_{vw}. \tag{9.1}$$

Note that Dijkstra scores are defined on the *edges*—a vertex $w \notin X$ may be the head of many different edges crossing from X to $V - X$, and these edges will typically have different Dijkstra scores.

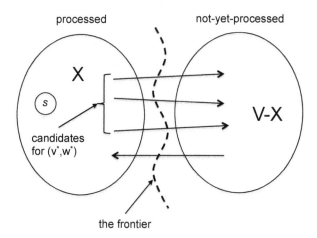

Figure 9.1: Every iteration of Dijkstra's algorithm processes one new vertex, the head of an edge crossing from X to $V - X$.

You can associate the Dijkstra score for an edge (v, w) with $v \in X$ and $w \notin X$ with the hypothesis that the shortest path from s to w consists of a shortest path from s to v (which hopefully has length $len(v)$) with the edge (v, w) (which has length ℓ_{vw}) tacked on at the end. Thus, the Dijkstra algorithm chooses to add the as-yet-unprocessed vertex that appears closest to s, according to the already-computed shortest-path distances and the lengths of the edges crossing from X to $V - X$. While adding w^* to X, the algorithm assigns $len(w^*)$ to its hypothesized shortest-path distance from s, which is the Dijkstra score $len(v^*) + \ell_{v^* w^*}$ of the edge (v^*, w^*). The magic of Dijkstra's algorithm, formalized in Theorem 9.1 below, is that this hypothesis is guaranteed to be correct, even if the algorithm has thus far looked at only a tiny fraction of the graph.[5]

9.2.2   An Example

Let's try out the `Dijkstra` algorithm on the example from Quiz 9.1:

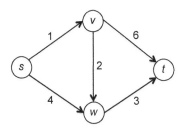

Initially, the set X contains only s, and $len(s) = 0$. In the first iteration of the main loop, there are two edges crossing from X to $V-X$ (and hence eligible to play the role of (v^*, w^*)), the edges (s, v) and (s, w). The Dijkstra scores (defined in (9.1)) for these two edges are $len(s) + \ell_{sv} = 0 + 1 = 1$ and $len(s) + \ell_{sw} = 0 + 4 = 4$. Because the former edge has the lower score, its head v is added to X, and $len(v)$ is assigned to the Dijkstra score of the edge (s, v), which is 1. In the second iteration, with $X = \{s, v\}$, there are three edges to consider for the role of (v^*, w^*): (s, w), (v, w), and (v, t). Their Dijkstra scores are $0 + 4 = 4$, $1 + 2 = 3$, and $1 + 6 = 7$. Because (v, w) has the lowest Dijkstra score, w gets sucked into X and $len(w)$ is assigned the value 3 ((v, w)'s Dijkstra score). We already know which vertex gets added to X in the final iteration (the only not-yet-processed vertex t), but we still need to determine the edge that leads to its addition (to compute $len(t)$). As (v, t) and (w, t) have Dijkstra scores

---

[5]To compute the shortest paths themselves (and not just their lengths), associate a pointer *predecessor*(v) with each vertex $v \in V$. When an edge (v^*, w^*) is chosen in an iteration of the main while loop (lines 4–6), assign *predecessor*(w^*) to v^*, the vertex responsible for w^*'s selection. After the algorithm concludes, to reconstruct a shortest path from s to a vertex v, follow the *predecessor* pointers backward from v until you reach s.

$1 + 6 = 7$ and $3 + 3 = 6$, respectively, $len(t)$ is set to the lower score of 6. The set X now contains all the vertices, so no edges cross from X to $V - X$ and the algorithm halts. The values $len(s) = 0$, $len(v) = 1$, $len(w) = 3$, and $len(t) = 6$ match the true shortest-path distances that we identified in Quiz 9.1.

Of course, the fact that an algorithm works correctly on a specific example does *not* imply that it is correct in general![6] In fact, the `Dijkstra` algorithm need *not* compute the correct shortest-path distances when edges can have negative lengths (Section 9.3.1). You should be initially skeptical of the `Dijkstra` algorithm and demand a proof that, at least in graphs with nonnegative edge lengths, it correctly solves the single-source shortest path problem.

*9.3   Why Is Dijkstra's Algorithm Correct?

9.3.1   A Bogus Reduction

You might be wondering why it matters whether or not edges have negative edge lengths. Can't we just force all the edge lengths to be nonnegative by adding a big number to every edge's length?

This is a great question—you should always be on the lookout for reductions to problems you already know how to solve. Alas, you cannot reduce the single-source shortest path problem with general edge lengths to the special case of nonnegative edge lengths in this way. The problem is that different paths from one vertex to another might not have the same number of edges. If we add some number to the length of each edge, then the lengths of different paths can increase by different amounts, and a shortest path in the new graph might be different than in the original graph. Here's a simple example:

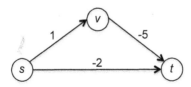

There are two paths from s to t: the direct path (which has length -2) and the two-hop path $s \to v \to t$ (which has length $1 + (-5) = -4$).

---

[6]Even a broken analog clock is correct two times a day. . .

The latter has the smaller (that is, more negative) length, and is the shortest s-t path.

To force the graph to have nonnegative edge lengths, we could add 5 to every edge's length:

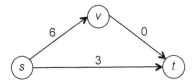

The shortest path from s to t has switched, and is now the direct s-t edge (which has length 3, better than the alternative of 6). Running a shortest-path algorithm on the transformed graph would not produce a correct answer for the original graph.

9.3.2   A Bad Example for the `Dijkstra` Algorithm

What happens if we try running the `Dijkstra` algorithm directly on a graph with some negative edge lengths, like the graph above? As always, initially $X = \{s\}$ and $len(s) = 0$, all of which is fine. In the first iteration of the main loop, however, the algorithm computes the Dijkstra scores of the edges (s, v) and (s, t), which are $len(s) + \ell_{sv} = 0 + 1 = 1$ and $len(s) + \ell_{st} = 0 + (-2) = -2$. The latter edge has the smaller score, and so the algorithm adds the vertex t to X and assigns $len(t)$ to the score -2. As we already noted, the actual shortest path from s to t (the path $s \to v \to t$) has length -4. We conclude that the `Dijkstra` algorithm need not compute the correct shortest-path distances in the presence of negative edge lengths.

9.3.3   Correctness with Nonnegative Edge Lengths

Proofs of correctness can feel pretty pedantic. That's why I often gloss over them for the algorithms for which students tend to have strong and accurate intuition. Dijkstra's algorithm is different. First, the fact that it doesn't work on extremely simple graphs with negative edge lengths (Section 9.3.1) should make you nervous. Second, the Dijkstra score (9.1) might seem mysterious or even arbitrary—why is it so important? Because of these doubts, and because it is such a fundamental algorithm, we'll take the time to carefully prove its correctness (in graphs with nonnegative edge lengths).

Theorem 9.1 (Correctness of `Dijkstra`**)** *For   every   directed graph $G = (V, E)$, every starting vertex s, and every choice of nonnegative edge lengths, at the conclusion of* `Dijkstra`*, $len(v) = dist(s, v)$ for every vertex $v \in V$.*

Induction Detour

The plan is to justify the shortest-path distances computed by the `Dijkstra` algorithm one by one, by induction on the number of iterations of its main loop. Recall that proofs by induction follow a fairly rigid template, with the goal of establishing that an assertion $P(k)$ holds for every positive integer k. In the proof of Theorem 9.1, we will define $P(k)$ as the statement: "for the kth vertex v added to the set X in `Dijkstra`, $len(v) = dist(s, v)$."

Analogous to a recursive algorithm, a proof by induction has two parts: a *base case* and an *inductive step*. The base case proves directly that $P(1)$ is true. In the inductive step, you assume that $P(1), \ldots, P(k-1)$ are all true—this is called the *inductive hypothesis*—and use this assumption to prove that $P(k)$ is consequently true as well. If you prove both the base case and the inductive step, then $P(k)$ is indeed true for every positive integer k. $P(1)$ is true by the base case, and applying the inductive step over and over again shows that $P(k)$ is true for arbitrarily large values of k.

On Reading Proofs

Mathematical arguments derive conclusions from assumptions. When reading a proof, always make sure you understand how each of the assumptions is used in the argument, and why the argument would break down in the absence of each assumption.

With this in mind, watch carefully for the role played in the proof of Theorem 9.1 by the two key assumptions: that edge lengths are nonnegative, and that the algorithm always chooses the edge with the smallest Dijkstra score. Any purported proof of Theorem 9.1 that fails to use both assumptions is automatically flawed.

Proof of Theorem 9.1

We proceed by induction, with $P(k)$ the assertion that the `Dijkstra` algorithm correctly computes the shortest-path distance of the kth vertex added to the set X. For the base case $(k = 1)$, we know that the first vertex added to X is the starting vertex s. The `Dijkstra` algorithm assigns 0 to $len(s)$. Because every edge has a nonnegative length, the shortest path from s to itself is the empty path, with length 0. Thus, $len(s) = 0 = dist(s, s)$, which proves $P(1)$.

For the inductive step, choose $k > 1$ and assume that $P(1), \dots, P(k-1)$ are all true—that $len(v) = dist(s, v)$ for the first $k - 1$ vertices v added by `Dijkstra` to X. Let w^* denote the kth vertex added to X, and let (v^*, w^*) denote the edge chosen in the corresponding iteration (necessarily with v^* already in X). The algorithm assigns $len(w^*)$ to the Dijkstra score of this edge, which is $len(v^*) + \ell_{v^* w^*}$. We're hoping that this value is the same as the true shortest-path distance $dist(s, w^*)$, but is it?

We argue in two parts that it is. First, let's prove that the true distance $dist(s, w^*)$ can only be less than the algorithm's speculation $len(w^*)$, with $dist(s, w^*) \leq len(w^*)$. Because v^* was already in X when the edge (v^*, w^*) was chosen, it was one of the first $k - 1$ vertices added to X. By the inductive hypothesis, the `Dijkstra` algorithm correctly computed v^*'s shortest-path distance: $len(v^*) = dist(s, v^*)$. In particular, there is a path P from s to v^* with length exactly $len(v^*)$. Tacking the edge (v^*, w^*) on at the end of P produces a path P^* from s to w^* with length $len(v^*) + \ell_{v^* w^*} = len(w^*)$ (Figure 9.2). The length of a shortest s-w^* path is no longer than that of the candidate path P^*, so $dist(s, w^*)$ is at most $len(w^*)$.

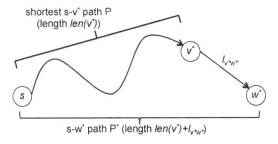

Figure 9.2: Tacking the edge (v^*, w^*) on at the end of a shortest s-v^* path P produces an s-w^* path P^* with length $len(v) + \ell_{v^* w^*}$.

Now for the reverse inequality, stating that $dist(s, w^*) \geq len(w^*)$ (and so $len(w^*) = dist(s, w^*)$, as desired). In other words, let's show that the path P^* in Figure 9.2 really is a shortest s-w^* path—that the length of every competing s-w^* path is at least $len(w^*)$.

Fix a competing s-w^* path P'. We know very little about P'. However, we *do* know that it originates at s and ends at w^*, and that s but not w^* belonged to the set X at the beginning of this iteration. Because it starts in X and ends outside X, the path P' crosses the frontier between X and $V - X$ at least once (Figure 9.3); let (y, z) denote the first edge of P' that crosses the frontier (with $y \in X$ and $z \notin X$).[7]

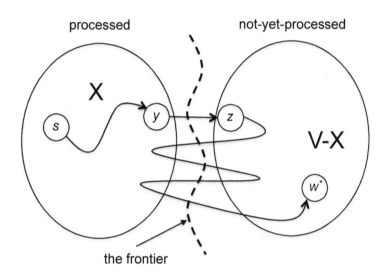

Figure 9.3: Every s-w^* path crosses at least once from X to $V - X$.

To argue that the length of P' is at least $len(w^*)$, we consider its three pieces separately: the initial part of P' that travels from s to y, the edge (y, z), and the final part that travels from z to w^*. The first part can't be shorter than a shortest path from s to y, so its length is at least $dist(s, y)$. The length of the edge (y, z) is ℓ_{yz}. We don't know much about the final part of the path, which ambles among vertices that the algorithm hasn't looked at yet. But we do know—because all edge lengths are nonnegative!—that its total length is at least zero:

---

[7]No worries if $y = s$ or $z = w^*$—the argument works fine, as you should check.

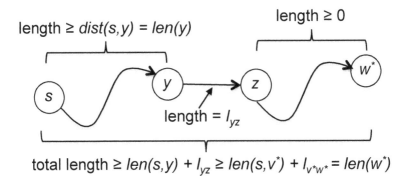

$$\text{total length} \geq len(s,y) + l_{yz} \geq len(s,v^*) + l_{v^*w^*} = len(w^*)$$

Combining our length lower bounds for the three parts of P', we have

$$\text{length of } P' \geq \underbrace{dist(s,y)}_{\text{s-y subpath}} + \underbrace{\ell_{yz}}_{\text{edge }(y,z)} + \underbrace{0}_{z\text{-}w^* \text{ subpath}} . \qquad (9.2)$$

The last order of business is to connect our length lower bound in (9.2) to the Dijkstra scores that guide the algorithm's decisions. Because $y \in X$, it was one of the first $k-1$ vertices added to X, and the inductive hypothesis implies that the algorithm correctly computed its shortest-path distance: $dist(s,y) = len(y)$. Thus, the inequality (9.2) translates to

$$\text{length of } P' \geq \underbrace{len(y) + \ell_{yz}}_{\text{Dijkstra score of edge }(y,z)} . \qquad (9.3)$$

The right-hand side is exactly the Dijkstra score of the edge (y,z). Because the algorithm always chooses the edge with the smallest Dijkstra score, and because it chose (v^*, w^*) over (y,z) in this iteration, the former has an even smaller Dijkstra score: $len(v^*) + \ell_{v^*w^*} \leq len(y) + \ell_{yz}$. Plugging this inequality into (9.3) gives us what we want:

$$\text{length of } P' \geq \underbrace{len(v^*) + \ell_{v^*w^*}}_{\text{Dijkstra score of edge }(v^*, w^*)} = len(w^*).$$

This completes the second part of the inductive step, and we conclude that $len(v) = dist(s,v)$ for every vertex v that ever gets added to the set X.

For the final nail in the coffin, consider a vertex v that was never added to X. When the algorithm finished, $len(v) = +\infty$ and no edges crossed from X to $V - X$. This means no path exists from s to v in the input graph—such a path would have to cross the frontier at some point—and, hence, $dist(s, v) = +\infty$ as well. We conclude that the algorithm halts with $len(v) = dist(s, v)$ for every vertex v, whether or not v was ever added to X. This completes the proof! $\mathcal{QED}$

9.4   Implementation and Running Time

Dijkstra's shortest-path algorithm is reminiscent of our linear-time graph search algorithms in Chapter 8. A key reason why breadth- and depth-first search run in linear time (Theorems 8.2 and 8.5) is that they spend only a constant amount of time deciding which vertex to explore next (by removing the vertex from the front of a queue or stack). Alarmingly, every iteration of Dijkstra's algorithm must identify the edge crossing the frontier with the smallest Dijkstra score. Can we still implement the algorithm in linear time?

Quiz 9.2

Which of the following running times best describes a straightforward implementation of Dijkstra's algorithm for graphs in adjacency-list representation? As usual, n and m denote the number of vertices and edges, respectively, of the input graph.

a) $O(m + n)$

b) $O(m \log n)$

c) $O(n^2)$

d) $O(mn)$

(See below for the solution and discussion.)

Correct answer: (d).   A straightforward implementation keeps track of which vertices are in X by associating a Boolean variable with each vertex. Each iteration, it performs an exhaustive search through all the edges, computes the Dijkstra score for each edge with tail in X and head outside X (in constant time per edge), and returns the crossing edge with the smallest score (or correctly identifies that no crossing edges exist). After at most $n-1$ iterations, the `Dijkstra` algorithm runs out of new vertices to add to its set X. Because the number of iterations is $O(n)$ and each takes time $O(m)$, the overall running time is $O(mn)$.

Proposition 9.2 (`Dijkstra` Running Time (Straightforward))
For every directed graph $G = (V, E)$, every starting vertex s, and every choice of nonnegative edge lengths, the straightforward implementation of `Dijkstra` runs in $O(mn)$ time, where $m = |E|$ and $n = |V|$.

The running time of the straightforward implementation is good but not great. It would work fine for graphs in which the number of vertices is in the hundreds or low thousands, but would choke on significantly larger graphs. Can we do better? The holy grail in algorithm design is a linear-time algorithm (or close to it), and this is what we want for the single-source shortest path problem. Such an algorithm could process graphs with millions of vertices on a commodity laptop.

We don't need a better *algorithm* to achieve a near-linear-time solution to the problem, just a better *implementation* of Dijkstra's algorithm. Data structures (queues and stacks) played a crucial role in our linear-time implementations of breadth- and depth-first search; analogously, Dijkstra's algorithm can be implemented in near-linear time with the assistance of the right data structure to facilitate the repeated minimum computations in its main loop. This data structure is called a *heap*, and it is the subject of the next chapter.

The Upshot

☆ In the single-source shortest path problem, the input consists of a graph, a starting vertex, and a length for each edge. The goal is to compute the length of a shortest path from the starting vertex to every other vertex.

☆ Dijkstra's algorithm processes vertices one by one, always choosing the not-yet-processed vertex that appears to be closest to the starting vertex.

⭐ An inductive argument proves that Dijkstra's algorithm correctly solves the single-source shortest path problem whenever the input graph has only nonnegative edge lengths.

⭐ Dijkstra's algorithm need not correctly solve the single-source shortest path problem when some edges of the input graph have negative lengths.

⭐ A straightforward implementation of Dijkstra's algorithm runs in $O(mn)$ time, where m and n denote the number of edges and vertices of the input graph, respectively.

Test Your Understanding

Problem 9.1 Consider a directed graph G with distinct and nonnegative edge lengths. Let s be a starting vertex and t a destination vertex, and assume that G has at least one s-t path. Which of the following statements are true? (Choose all that apply.)

a) The shortest (meaning minimum-length) s-t path might have as many as $n - 1$ edges, where n is the number of vertices.

b) There is a shortest s-t path with no repeated vertices (that is, with no loops).

c) The shortest s-t path must include the minimum-length edge of G.

d) The shortest s-t path must exclude the maximum-length edge of G.

Problem 9.2 *(S)* Consider a directed graph G with a starting vertex s, a destination t, and nonnegative edge lengths. Under what conditions is the shortest s-t path guaranteed to be unique?

a) When all edge lengths are distinct positive integers.

b) When all edge lengths are distinct powers of 2.

c) When all edge lengths are distinct positive integers and the graph G contains no directed cycles.

d) None of the other options are correct.

Problem 9.3 *(S)* Consider a directed graph G with nonnegative edge lengths and two distinct vertices, s and t. Let P denote a shortest path from s to t. If we add 10 to the length of every edge in the graph, then: (Choose all that apply.)

a) P definitely remains a shortest s-t path.

b) P definitely does not remain a shortest s-t path.

c) P might or might not remain a shortest s-t path (depending on the graph).

d) If P has only one edge, then P definitely remains a shortest s-t path.

Problem 9.4 Consider a directed graph G and a starting vertex s with the following properties: no edges enter the starting vertex s; edges that leave s have arbitrary (possibly negative) lengths; and all other edge lengths are nonnegative. Does Dijkstra's algorithm correctly solve the single-source shortest path problem in this case? (Choose all that apply.)

a) Yes, for all such inputs.

b) Never, for no such inputs.

c) Maybe, maybe not (depending on the specific choice of G, s, and edge lengths).

d) Only if we add the assumption that G contains no directed cycles with negative total length.

Problem 9.5 Consider a directed graph G and a starting vertex s. Suppose G has some negative edge lengths but no negative cycles, meaning G does not have a directed cycle in which the sum of its edge lengths is negative. Suppose you run Dijkstra's algorithm on this input. Which of the following statements are true? (Choose all that apply.)

a) Dijkstra's algorithm might loop forever.

b) It's impossible to run Dijkstra's algorithm on a graph with negative edge lengths.

c) Dijkstra's algorithm always halts, but in some cases the shortest-path distances it computes will not all be correct.

d) Dijkstra's algorithm always halts, and in some cases the shortest-path distances it computes will all be correct.

Problem 9.6 Continuing the previous problem, suppose now that the input graph G does contain a negative cycle, and also a path from the starting vertex s to this cycle. Suppose you run Dijkstra's algorithm on this input. Which of the following statements are true? (Choose all that apply.)

a) Dijkstra's algorithm might loop forever.

b) It's impossible to run Dijkstra's algorithm on a graph with a negative cycle.

c) Dijkstra's algorithm always halts, but in some cases the shortest-path distances it computes will not all be correct.

d) Dijkstra's algorithm always halts, and in some cases the shortest-path distances it computes will all be correct.

Challenge Problems

Problem 9.7 *(S)* Consider a directed graph $G = (V, E)$ with non-negative edge lengths and a starting vertex s. Define the *bottleneck* of a path to be the maximum length of one of its edges (as opposed to the sum of the lengths of its edges). Show how to modify Dijkstra's algorithm to compute, for each vertex $v \in V$, the smallest bottleneck of any s-v path. Your algorithm should run in $O(mn)$ time, where m and n denote the number of edges and vertices, respectively.

Programming Problems

Problem 9.8 Implement in your favorite programming language the `Dijkstra` algorithm from Section 9.2, and use it to solve the single-source shortest path problem in different directed graphs. With the straightforward implementation in this chapter, what's the size of the largest problem you can solve in five minutes or less? (See `www.algorithmsilluminated.org` for test cases and challenge data sets.)

Chapter 10

The Heap Data Structure

The remaining three chapters of this book are about three of the most important and ubiquitous data structures out there—heaps, search trees, and hash tables. The goals are to learn the operations that these data structures support (along with their running times), to develop through example applications your intuition about which data structures are useful for which sorts of problems, and optionally, to learn a bit about how they are implemented under the hood.[1] We begin with *heaps*, a data structure that facilitates fast minimum or maximum computations.

10.1 Data Structures: An Overview

10.1.1 Choosing the Right Data Structure

Data structures are used in almost every major piece of software, so knowing when and how to use them is an essential skill for the serious programmer. The raison d'être of a data structure is to organize data so you can access it quickly and usefully. You've already seen a few examples. The *queue* data structure, used in our linear-time implementation of breadth-first search (Section 8.2), sequentially organizes data so that removing an object from the front or adding an object to the back takes constant time. The *stack* data structure, which was crucial in our iterative implementation of depth-first search (Section 8.4), lets you remove an object from or add an object to the front in constant time.

There are many more data structures out there—in this book series, we'll see heaps, binary search trees, hash tables, bloom filters, and (in

---

[1]Some programmers reserve the phrase *data structure* for a concrete implementation, and refer to the list of supported operations as an *abstract data type*.

Part 3) union-find. Why such a bewildering laundry list? Because *different data structures support different sets of operations, making them well-suited for different types of programming tasks.* For example, breadth- and depth-first search have different needs, necessitating two different data structures. Our fast implementation of Dijkstra's shortest-path algorithm (in Section 10.4) has still different needs, requiring the more sophisticated heap data structure.

What are the pros and cons of different data structures, and how should you choose which one to use in a program? In general, the more operations a data structure supports, the slower the operations and the greater the space overhead. The following quote, widely attributed to Albert Einstein, is germane:

"Make things as simple as possible, but not simpler."

When implementing a program, it's important that you think carefully about exactly which operations you'll use over and over again. For example, do you care only about tracking which objects are stored in a data structure, or do you also want them ordered in a specific way? Once you understand your program's needs, you can follow the principle of parsimony and choose a data structure that supports all the desired operations and no superfluous ones.

Principle of Parsimony

Choose the simplest data structure that supports all the operations required by your application.

10.1.2   Taking It to the Next Level

What are your current and desired levels of expertise in data structures?

(Level 0:) "What's a data structure?"

Level 0 is total ignorance—someone who has never heard of a data structure and is unaware that cleverly organizing your data can dramatically improve a program's running time.

(Level 1:) "I hear good things about hash tables."

Level 1 is cocktail party-level awareness—at this level, you could at least have a conversation about basic data structures.[2] You have heard of several basic structures like search trees and hash tables, and are perhaps aware of some of their supported operations, but would be shaky trying to use them in a program or a technical interview.

(Level 2:) "This problem calls out for a heap."

With level 2, we're starting to get somewhere. This is someone who has solid literacy about basic data structures, is comfortable using them as a client in their own programs, and has a good sense of which data structures are appropriate for which types of programming tasks.

(Level 3:) "I use only data structures that I wrote myself."

Level 3, the most advanced level, is for hardcore programmers and computer scientists who are not content to merely use existing data structure implementations as a client. At this level, you have a detailed understanding of the guts of basic data structures, and exactly how they are implemented.

The biggest marginal empowerment comes from reaching level 2. Most programmers will, at some point, need to be educated clients of basic data structures like heaps, search trees, and hash tables. The primary goal of Chapters 10–12 is to bring you up to this level with these data structures, with a focus on the operations they support and their canonical applications. All these data structures are readily available in the standard libraries of most modern programming languages, waiting to be deftly deployed in your own programs.

Advanced programmers do sometimes need to implement a customized version of one of these data structures from scratch. Each of Chapters 10–12 includes at least one advanced section on typical implementations of these data structures. These sections are for those of you wanting to up your game to level 3.

---

[2]Speaking, as always, about sufficiently nerdy cocktail parties!

10.2 Supported Operations

A *heap* is a data structure that keeps track of an evolving set of objects with *keys* and can quickly identify the object with the smallest key.[3] For example, objects might correspond to employee records, with keys equal to their identification numbers. They might be the edges of a graph, with keys corresponding to edge lengths. Or they could correspond to events scheduled for the future, with each key indicating the time at which the event will occur.[4]

10.2.1 Insert and Extract-Min

The most important things to remember about any data structure are the operations it supports and the time required for each. The two most important operations supported by heaps are the INSERT and EXTRACTMIN operations.[5]

Heaps: Basic Operations

INSERT: given a heap H and a new object x, add x to H.

EXTRACTMIN: given a heap H, remove and return from H an object with the smallest key (or a pointer to it).

For example, if you invoke INSERT four times to add objects with keys 12, 7, 29, and 15 to an empty heap, the EXTRACTMIN operation will return the object with key 7. Keys need not be distinct; if there is more than one object in a heap with the smallest key, the EXTRACTMIN operation returns an arbitrary such object.

It would be easy to support only the INSERT operation, by repeatedly tacking on new objects to the end of an array or linked list (in constant time). The catch is that EXTRACTMIN would require a linear-time exhaustive search through all the objects. It's also clear how to support only EXTRACTMIN—sort the initial set of n objects by key once and for all up front (using $O(n \log n)$ preprocessing time),

---

[3]Not to be confused with heap *memory*, the part of a program's memory reserved for dynamic allocation.

[4]Keys are often numerical but can belong to any totally ordered set—what matters is that for every pair of non-equal keys, one is less than the other.

[5]Data structures supporting these operations are also called *priority queues*.

and then successive calls to EXTRACTMIN peel off objects from the beginning of the sorted list one by one (each in constant time). Here the catch is that any straightforward implementation of INSERT requires linear time (as you should check). The trick is to design a data structure that enables *both* operations to run super-quickly. This is exactly the raison d'être of heaps.

Standard implementations of heaps, like the one outlined in Section 10.5, provide the following guarantee.

Theorem 10.1 (Running Time of Basic Heap Operations)
In a heap with n objects, the INSERT *and* EXTRACTMIN *operations run in* $O(\log n)$ *time.*

As a bonus, in typical implementations, the constant hidden by the big-O notation is very small, and there is almost no extra space overhead.

There's also a heap variant that supports the INSERT and EXTRACTMAX operations in $O(\log n)$ time, where n is the number of objects. One way to implement this variant is to switch the direction of all the inequalities in the implementation in Section 10.5. A second way is to use a standard heap but negate the keys of objects before inserting them (which effectively transforms EXTRACTMIN into EXTRACTMAX). Neither variant of a heap supports both EXTRACTMIN and EXTRACTMAX simultaneously in $O(\log n)$ time—you have to pick which one you want.[6]

10.2.2   Additional Operations

Heaps can also support a number of less essential operations.

Heaps: Extra Operations

FINDMIN: given a heap H, return an object with the smallest key (or a pointer to it).

HEAPIFY: given objects $x_1, \ldots, x_n$, create a heap containing them.

---

[6]If you want both, you can use one heap of each type (see also Section 10.3.3), or upgrade to a balanced binary search tree (see Chapter 11).

DELETE: given a heap H and a pointer to an object x in H,
delete x from H.

You could simulate a FINDMIN operation by invoking EXTRACT-MIN and then applying INSERT to the result (in $O(\log n)$ time, by Theorem 10.1), but a typical heap implementation can avoid this circuitous solution and support FINDMIN directly in $O(1)$ time. You could implement HEAPIFY by inserting the n objects one by one into an empty heap (in $O(n \log n)$ total time, by Theorem 10.1), but there's a slick way to add n objects to an empty heap in a batch in total time $O(n)$. Finally, heaps can also support deletions of arbitrary objects—not just an object with the smallest key—in $O(\log n)$ time (see also Programming Project 10.8).

Theorem 10.2 (Running Time of Extra Heap Operations)
In a heap with n objects, the FINDMIN, HEAPIFY, and DELETE operations run in $O(1)$, $O(n)$, and $O(\log n)$ time, respectively.

Summarizing, here's the final scorecard for heaps:

Operation	Running time
INSERT	$O(\log n)$
EXTRACTMIN	$O(\log n)$
FINDMIN	$O(1)$
HEAPIFY	$O(n)$
DELETE	$O(\log n)$

Table 10.1: Heaps: supported operations and their running times, where n denotes the current number of objects stored in the heap.

When to Use a Heap

If your application requires fast minimum (or maximum) computations on a dynamically changing set of objects, the heap is usually the data structure of choice.

10.3   Applications

The next order of business is to walk through several example applications and develop a feel for what heaps are good for. The common
theme of these applications is the replacement of minimum computations, naively implemented using (linear-time) exhaustive search,
with a sequence of (logarithmic-time) EXTRACTMIN operations from
a heap. Whenever you see an algorithm or program with lots of
brute-force minimum or maximum computations, a light bulb should
go off in your head: *This calls out for a heap!*

10.3.1   Application: Sorting

For our first application, let's return to the mother of all computational
problems, *sorting*.

Problem: Sorting

Input: An array of n numbers, in arbitrary order.

Output: An array of the same numbers, sorted from smallest to largest.

For example, given the input array

5	4	1	8	7	2	6	3

the desired output array is

1	2	3	4	5	6	7	8

Perhaps the simplest sorting algorithm is `SelectionSort`. This
algorithm performs a linear scan through the input array to identify
the minimum element, swaps it with the first element in the array,
does a second scan over the remaining $n - 1$ elements to identify and
swap into the second position the second-smallest element, and so
on. Each scan takes time proportional to the number of remaining

elements, so the overall running time is $\Theta(\sum_{i=1}^{n} i) = \Theta(n^2)$.[7] Because each iteration of `SelectionSort` computes a minimum element using exhaustive search, it calls out for a heap! The idea is simple: Insert all the elements in the input array into a heap, and populate the output array from left to right with successively extracted minimum elements. The first extraction produces the smallest element; the second the smallest remaining element (the second-smallest overall); and so on.

HeapSort

Input: array A of n distinct integers.
Output: array B with the same integers, sorted from smallest to largest.

$H :=$ empty heap
for $i = 1$ to n **do**
    INSERT $A[i]$ into H
for $i = 1$ to n **do**
    $B[i] :=$ EXTRACTMIN from H

Quiz 10.1

What's the running time of `HeapSort`, as a function of the length n of the input array?

a) $O(n)$

b) $O(n \log n)$

c) $O(n^2)$

d) $O(n^2 \log n)$

(See below for the solution and discussion.)

---

[7]The sum $\sum_{i=1}^{n} i$ is at most n^2 (it has n terms, each at most n) and at least $n^2/4$ (it has $n/2$ terms that are all at least $n/2$).

Correct answer: (b). The work done by HeapSort boils down to $2n$ operations on a heap containing at most n objects.[8] Because Theorem 10.1 guarantees that every heap operation requires $O(\log n)$ time, the overall running time is $O(n \log n)$.

Theorem 10.3 (Running Time of HeapSort) *For every input array of length $n \geq 1$, the running time of HeapSort is $O(n \log n)$.*

Let's take a step back and appreciate what just happened. We started with the least imaginative sorting algorithm possible, the quadratic-time SelectionSort algorithm. We recognized the pattern of repeated minimum computations, swapped in a heap data structure, and—boom!—out popped an $O(n \log n)$-time sorting algorithm.[9] This is a great running time for a sorting algorithm—it's even *optimal*, up to constant factors, among comparison-based sorting algorithms.[10] A neat byproduct of this observation is a proof that there's no comparison-based way to implement both the INSERT and EXTRACTMIN operations in better-than-logarithmic time: such a solution would yield a better-than-$O(n \log n)$-time comparison-based sorting algorithm, and we know this is impossible.

10.3.2   Application: Event Manager

Our second application, while a bit obvious, is both canonical and practical. Imagine you've been tasked with writing software that performs a simulation of the physical world. For example, perhaps you're contributing to a basketball video game. For the simulation,

---

[8] An even better implementation would replace the first loop with a single HEAPIFY operation, which runs in $O(n)$ time. The second loop still requires $O(n \log n)$ time, however.

[9] For clarity we described HeapSort using separate input and output arrays, but it can be implemented in place, with almost no additional memory. This in-place implementation is a super-practical algorithm, and is almost as fast as QuickSort in most applications.

[10] Recall from Section 5.6 of *Part 1* that a *comparison-based* sorting algorithm accesses the input array only via comparisons between pairs of elements, and never directly accesses the value of an element. "General-purpose" sorting algorithms, which make no assumptions about the elements to be sorted, are necessarily comparison-based. Examples include SelectionSort, InsertionSort, HeapSort, and QuickSort. Non-examples include BucketSort, CountingSort, and RadixSort. Theorem 5.5 from *Part 1* shows that no comparison-based sorting algorithm has a worst-case asymptotic running time better than $\Theta(n \log n)$.

you must keep track of different events and when they should occur—
the event that a player shoots the ball at a particular angle and
velocity, that the ball consequently hits the back of the rim, that two
players vie for the rebound at the same time, that one of these players
commits an over-the-back foul on the other, and so on.

A simulation must repeatedly identify what happens next. This
boils down to repeated minimum computations on the set of scheduled
event times, so a light bulb should go off in your head: The problem
calls out for a heap! If events are stored in a heap, with keys equal
to their scheduled times, the EXTRACTMIN operation hands you the
next event on a silver platter, in logarithmic time. New events can be
inserted into the heap as they arise (again, in logarithmic time).

10.3.3   Application: Median Maintenance

For a less obvious application of heaps, let's consider the *median
maintenance* problem. You are presented with a sequence of numbers,
one by one; assume for simplicity that they are distinct. Each time
you receive a new number, your responsibility is to reply with the
median element of all the numbers you've seen thus far.[11] Thus, after
seeing the first 11 numbers, you should reply with the sixth-smallest
one you've seen; after 12, the sixth- or seventh-smallest; after 13, the
seventh-smallest; and so on.

One approach to the problem, which should seem like overkill, is
to recompute the median from scratch in every iteration. We saw
in Chapter 6 of *Part 1* how to compute the median of a length-n
array in $O(n)$ time, so this solution requires $O(i)$ time in each round i.
Alternatively, we could keep the elements seen so far in a sorted array,
so that it's easy to compute the median element in constant time.
The drawback is that updating the sorted array when a new number
arrives can require linear time. Can we do better?

Using heaps, we can solve the median maintenance problem in
just *logarithmic* time per round. I suggest putting the book down
at this point and spending several minutes thinking about how this
might be done.

---

[11]Recall that the *median* of a collection of numbers is its "middle element." In
an array with odd length $2k - 1$, the median is the kth order statistic (that is,
the kth-smallest element). In an array with even length $2k$, both the kth and
$(k + 1)$th order statistics are considered median elements.

The key idea is to maintain *two* heaps H_1 and H_2 while satisfying two invariants.[12] The first invariant is that H_1 and H_2 are *balanced*, meaning they each contain the same number of elements (after an even round) or that one contains exactly one more element than the other (after an odd round). The second invariant is that H_1 and H_2 are *ordered*, meaning every element in H_1 is smaller than every element in H_2. For example, if the numbers so far have been $1, 2, 3, 4, 5$, then H_1 stores 1 and 2 and H_2 stores 4 and 5; the median element 3 is allowed to go in either one, as either the maximum element of H_1 or the minimum element of H_2. If we've seen $1, 2, 3, 4, 5, 6$, then the first three numbers are in H_1 and the second three are in H_2; both the maximum element of H_1 and the minimum element of H_2 are median elements. One twist: H_2 will be a standard heap, supporting INSERT and EXTRACTMIN, while H_1 will be the "max" variant described in Section 10.2.1, supporting INSERT and EXTRACTMAX. This way, we can extract the median element with one heap operation, whether it's in H_1 or H_2.

We still must explain how to update H_1 and H_2 each time a new element arrives so that they remain balanced and ordered. To figure out where to insert a new element x so that the heaps remain ordered, it's enough to compute the maximum element y in H_1 and the minimum element z in H_2.[13] If x is less than y, it has to go in H_1; if it's more than z, it has to go in H_2; if it's in between, it can go in either one. Do H_1 and H_2 stay balanced even after x is inserted? Yes, except for one case: In an even round $2k$, if x is inserted into the bigger heap (with k elements), this heap will contain $k + 1$ elements while the other contains only $k - 1$ elements (Figure 10.1(a)). But this imbalance is easy to fix: Extract the maximum or minimum element from H_1 or H_2, respectively (whichever contains more elements), and re-insert this element into the other heap (Figure 10.1(b)). The two heaps stay ordered (as you should check) and are now balanced as well. This solution uses a constant number of heap operations each round, for a running time of $O(\log i)$ in round i.

---

[12] An *invariant* of an algorithm is a property that is always true at prescribed points of its execution (like at the end of every loop iteration).

[13] This can be done in logarithmic time by extracting and re-inserting these two elements. A better solution is to use the FINDMIN and FINDMAX operations, which run in constant time (see Section 10.2.2).

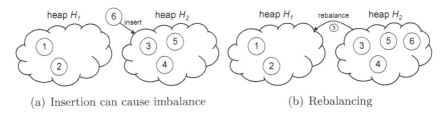

(a) Insertion can cause imbalance   (b) Rebalancing

Figure 10.1: When inserting a new element causes the heap H_2 to have two more elements than H_1, the smallest element in H_2 is extracted and re-inserted into H_1 to restore balance.

10.4 Speeding Up Dijkstra's Algorithm

Our final and most sophisticated application of heaps is a near linear-time implementation of Dijkstra's algorithm for the single-source shortest path problem (Chapter 9). This application vividly illustrates the beautiful interplay between the design of algorithms and the design of data structures.

10.4.1 Why Heaps?

We saw in Proposition 9.2 that the straightforward implementation of Dijkstra's algorithm requires $O(mn)$ time, where m is the number of edges and n is the number of vertices. This is fast enough to process medium-size graphs (with thousands of vertices and edges) but not big graphs (with millions of vertices and edges). Can we do better? Heaps enable a blazingly fast, near-linear-time implementation of Dijkstra's algorithm.

Theorem 10.4 (Dijkstra Running Time (Heap-Based)) *For every directed graph $G = (V, E)$, every starting vertex s, and every choice of nonnegative edge lengths, the heap-based implementation of Dijkstra runs in $O((m+n)\log n)$ time, where $m = |E|$ and $n = |V|$.*

While not quite as fast as our linear-time graph search algorithms, $O((m + n)\log n)$ is still a fantastic running time—comparable to our best sorting algorithms, and good enough to qualify as a for-free primitive.

   Let's remember how Dijkstra's algorithm works (Section 9.2). The algorithm maintains a subset $X \subseteq V$ of vertices to which it has already computed shortest-path distances. In every iteration, it identifies the edge crossing the frontier (with tail in X and head in $V - X$) with the minimum Dijkstra score, where the Dijkstra score of such an edge (v, w) is the (already computed) shortest-path distance $len(v)$ from the starting vertex to v plus the length ℓ_{vw} of the edge. In other words, every iteration of the main loop does a minimum computation, on the Dijkstra scores of the edges that cross the frontier. The straightforward implementation uses exhaustive search to perform these minimum computations. As speeding up minimum computations from linear time to logarithmic time is the raison d'être of heaps, at this point a light bulb should go off in your head: Dijkstra's algorithm calls out for a heap!

10.4.2   The Plan

What should we store in a heap, and what should their keys be? Your first thought might be to store the edges of the input graph in a heap, with an eye toward replacing the minimum computations (over edges) in the straightforward implementation with calls to EXTRACTMIN. This idea can be made to work, but the slicker and quicker implementation stores *vertices* in a heap. This might surprise you, as Dijkstra scores are defined for edges and not for vertices. On the flip side, we cared about edges' Dijkstra scores only inasmuch as they guided us to the vertex to process next. Can we use a heap to cut to the chase and directly compute this vertex?

The concrete plan is to store the as-yet-unprocessed vertices ($V - X$ in the Dijkstra pseudocode) in a heap, while maintaining the following invariant.

Invariant

The key of a vertex $w \in V - X$ is the minimum Dijkstra score of an edge with tail $v \in X$ and head w, or $+\infty$ if no such edge exists.

That is, we want the equation

$$key(w) = \min_{(v,w)\in E \,:\, v\in X} \underbrace{len(v) + \ell_{vw}}_{\text{Dijkstra score}} \tag{10.1}$$

to hold at all times for every $w \in V - X$, where $len(v)$ denotes the shortest-path distance of v computed in an earlier iteration of the algorithm (Figure 10.2).

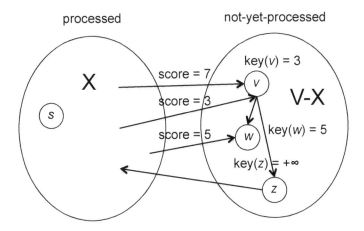

Figure 10.2: The key of a vertex $w \in V - X$ is defined as the minimum Dijkstra score of an edge with head w and tail in X.

What's going on? Imagine that we use a two-round knockout tournament to identify the edge (v, w) with $v \in X$ and $w \notin X$ with the minimum Dijkstra score. The first round comprises a local tournament for each vertex $w \in V - X$, where the participants are the edges (v, w) with $v \in X$ and head w, and the first-round winner is the participant with the smallest Dijkstra score (if any). The first-round winners (at most one per vertex $w \in V - X$) proceed to the second round, and the final champion is the first-round winner with the lowest Dijkstra score. This champion is the same edge that would be identified by exhaustive search.

The value of the key (10.1) of a vertex $w \in V - X$ is exactly the winning Dijkstra score in the local tournament at w, so our invariant effectively implements all the first-round competitions. Extracting the vertex with the minimum key then implements the second round of the tournament, and returns on a silver platter the next vertex to process, namely the head of the crossing edge with the smallest Dijkstra score. The point is, as long as we maintain our invariant, we can implement each iteration of Dijkstra's algorithm with a single heap operation.

The pseudocode looks like this:[14]

Dijkstra (Heap-Based, Part 1)

Input: directed graph $G = (V, E)$ in adjacency-list representation, a vertex $s \in V$, a length $\ell_e \geq 0$ for each $e \in E$.

Postcondition: for every vertex v, the value $len(v)$ equals the true shortest-path distance $dist(s, v)$.

```
// Initialization
1  X := empty set, H := empty heap
2  key(s) := 0
3  for every v ≠ s do
4     key(v) := +∞
5  for every v ∈ V do
6     INSERT v into H              // or use HEAPIFY
   // Main loop
7  while H is non-empty do
8     w* := EXTRACTMIN(H)
9     add w* to X
10    len(w*) := key(w*)
      // update heap to maintain invariant
11    (to be announced)
```

But how much work is it to maintain the invariant?

10.4.3   Maintaining the Invariant

Now it's time to pay the piper. We enjoyed the fruits of our invariant, which reduces each minimum computation required by Dijkstra's algorithm to a single heap operation. In exchange, we must explain how to maintain it without excessive work.

Each iteration of the algorithm moves one vertex v from $V - X$ to X, which changes the frontier (Figure 10.3). Edges from vertices

---

[14]Initializing the set X of processed vertices to the empty set rather than to the starting vertex leads to cleaner pseudocode (cf., Section 9.2.1). The first iteration of the main loop is guaranteed to extract the starting vertex (do you see why?), which is then the first vertex added to X.

in X to v get sucked into X and no longer cross the frontier. More
problematically, edges from v to other vertices of $V - X$ no longer
reside entirely in $V - X$ and instead cross from X to $V - X$. Why is
this a problem? Because our invariant (10.1) insists that, for every
vertex $w \in V - X$, w's key equals the smallest Dijkstra score of a
crossing edge ending at w. New crossing edges mean new candidates
for the smallest Dijkstra score, so the right-hand side of (10.1) might
decrease for some vertices w. For example, the first time a vertex v
with $(v, w) \in E$ gets sucked into X, this expression drops from $+\infty$
to a finite number (namely, $len(v) + \ell_{vw}$).

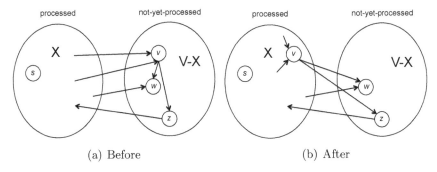

(a) Before   (b) After

Figure 10.3: When a new vertex v is moved from $V - X$ to X, edges
going out of v can become crossing edges.

Every time we extract a vertex w^* from the heap, moving it
from $V - X$ to X, we might need to decrease the key of some of the
vertices remaining in $V - X$ to reflect the new crossing edges. Because
all the new crossing edges emanate from w^*, we need only iterate
through w^*'s list of outgoing edges and check the vertices $y \in V - X$
with an edge (w^*, y). For each such vertex y, there are two candidates
for the first-round winner in y's local tournament: either it is the same
as before, or it is the new entrant (w^*, y). Thus, the new value of y's
key should be either its old value or the Dijkstra score $len(w^*) + \ell_{w^*y}$
of the new crossing edge, whichever is smaller.

How can we decrease the key of an object in a heap? One easy way
is to remove it, using the DELETE operation described in Section 10.2.2,
update its key, and use INSERT to add it back into the heap.[15] This

---

[15]Some heap implementations export a DECREASEKEY operation, running in

completes the heap-based implementation of the `Dijkstra` algorithm.

`Dijkstra` (Heap-Based, Part 2)

```
// update heap to maintain invariant
```
12   **for** every edge (w^*, y) **do**
13   DELETE y from H
14        $key(y) := \min\{key(y), len(w^*) + \ell_{w^*y}\}$
15   INSERT y into H

10.4.4   Running Time

Almost all the work performed by the heap-based implementation of `Dijkstra` consists of heap operations (as you should check). Each of these operations takes $O(\log n)$ time, where n is the number of vertices. (The heap never contains more than $n - 1$ objects.)

How many heap operations does the algorithm perform? There are $n - 1$ operations in each of lines 6 and 8—one per vertex other than the starting vertex s. What about in lines 13 and 15?

Quiz 10.2

How many times does `Dijkstra` execute lines 13 and 15? Select the smallest bound that applies. (As usual, n and m denote the number of vertices and edges, respectively.)

a) $O(n)$

b) $O(m)$

c) $O(n^2)$

d) $O(mn)$

(See below for the solution and discussion.)

$O(\log n)$ time for an n-object heap. In this case, only one heap operation is needed.

Correct answer: (b). Lines 13 and 15 may look a little scary. In one iteration of the main loop, these two lines might be performed as many as $n-1$ times—once per outgoing edge of w^*. There are $n-1$ iterations, which seems to lead to a quadratic number of heap operations. This bound is accurate for dense graphs, but in general, we can do better. The reason? Let's assign responsibility for these heap operations to *edges* rather than vertices. Each edge (v, w) of the graph makes at most one appearance in line 12—when v is first extracted from the heap and moved from $V - X$ to X.[16] Thus, lines 13 and 15 are each performed at most once per edge, for a total of $2m$ operations, where m is the number of edges.

Quiz 10.2 shows that the heap-based implementation of `Dijkstra` uses $O(m+n)$ heap operations, each taking $O(\log n)$ time. The overall running time is $O((m+n)\log n)$, as promised by Theorem 10.4. $\mathscr{QED}$

*10.5 Implementation Details

Let's take your understanding of heaps to the next level by describing how you would implement one from scratch. We'll focus on the two basic operations—INSERT and EXTRACTMIN—and how to ensure that both run in logarithmic time.

10.5.1 Heaps as Trees

There are two ways to visualize objects in a heap, as a tree (better for pictures and exposition) or as an array (better for an implementation). Let's start with trees.

A heap can be viewed as a rooted binary tree—where each node has 0, 1, or 2 children—in which every level is as full as possible. When the number of objects stored is one less than a power of 2, every level is full (Figures 10.4(a) and 10.4(b)). When the number of objects is between two such numbers, the only non-full layer is the last one, which is populated from left to right (Figure 10.4(c)).[17]

A heap manages objects associated with keys so that the following *heap property* holds.

---

[16]If w is extracted before v, the edge (v, w) never makes an appearance.

[17]For some reason, computer scientists seem to think that trees grow downward.

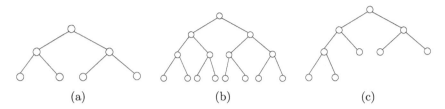

Figure 10.4: Full binary trees with 7, 15, and 9 nodes.

The Heap Property

For every object x, the key of x is less than or equal to the keys of its children.

Duplicate keys are allowed. For example, here's a valid heap containing nine objects:[18]

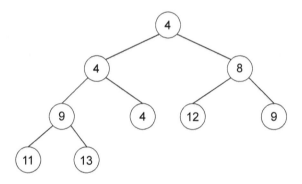

For every parent-child pair, the parent's key is at most that of the child.[19]

There's more than one way to arrange objects so that the heap property holds. Here's another heap, with the same set of keys:

---

[18] When we draw a heap, we show only the objects' keys. Don't forget that what a heap really stores is objects (or pointers to objects). Each object is associated with a key and possibly lots of other data.

[19] Applying the heap property iteratively to an object's children, its children's children, and so on shows that the key of each object is less than or equal to those of *all* of its direct descendants. The example above illustrates that the heap property implies nothing about the relative order of keys in different subtrees—just like in real family trees!

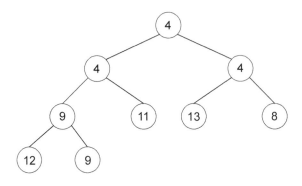

Both heaps have a "4" at the root, which is also (tied for) the smallest of all the keys. This is not an accident: because keys only decrease as you traverse a heap upward, the root's key is as small as it gets. This should sound encouraging, given that the raison d'être of a heap is fast minimum computations.

10.5.2   Heaps as Arrays

In our minds we visualize a heap as a tree, but in an implementation we use an array with length equal to the maximum number of objects we expect to store. The first element of the array corresponds to the tree's root, the next two elements to the next level of the tree (in the same order), and so on (Figure 10.5).

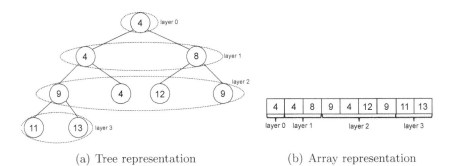

(a) Tree representation   (b) Array representation

Figure 10.5: Mapping the tree representation of a heap to its array representation.

Parent-child relationships in the tree translate nicely to the array (Table 10.2). Assuming the array positions are labeled $1, 2, \ldots, n$, where n is the number of objects, the children of the object in position i

correspond to the objects in positions $2i$ and $2i + 1$ (if any). For example, in Figure 10.5, the children of the root (in position 1) are the next two objects (in positions 2 and 3), the children of the 8 (in position 3) are the objects in positions 6 and 7, and so on. Going in reverse, for a non-root object (in position $i \geq 2$), i's parent is the object in position $\lfloor i/2 \rfloor$.[20] For example, in Figure 10.5, the parent of the last object (in position 9) is the object in position $\lfloor 9/2 \rfloor = 4$.

Position of parent	$\lfloor i/2 \rfloor$ (provided $i \geq 2$)
Position of left child	$2i$ (provided $2i \leq n$)
Position of right child	$2i + 1$ (provided $2i + 1 \leq n$)

Table 10.2: Relationships between the position $i \in \{1, 2, 3, \ldots, n\}$ of an object in a heap and the positions of its parent, left child, and right child, where n denotes the number of objects in the heap.

There are such simple formulas to go from a child to its parent and back because we use only full binary trees.[21] There is no need to explicitly store the tree; consequently, the heap data structure has minimal space overhead.[22]

10.5.3   Implementing INSERT in $O(\log n)$ Time

We'll illustrate the implementation of both the INSERT and EXTRACT-MIN operations by example rather than by pseudocode.[23] The challenge is to both keep the tree full and maintain the heap property after an object is added or removed. We'll follow the same blueprint for both operations:

1. Keep the tree full in the most obvious way possible.

2. Play whack-a-mole to systematically squash any violations of the heap property.

---

[20] The notation $\lfloor x \rfloor$ denotes the "floor" function, which rounds its argument down to the nearest integer.

[21] As a bonus, in low-level languages it's possible to multiply or divide by 2 ridiculously quickly, using bit-shifting tricks.

[22] By contrast, search trees (Chapter 11) need not be full; they require additional space to store explicit pointers from each node to its children.

[23] We'll keep drawing heaps as trees, but don't forget that they're stored as arrays. When we talk about going from a node to a child or its parent, we mean by applying the simple index formulas in Table 10.2.

Specifically, recall the INSERT operation:

given a heap H and a new object x, add x to H.

After x's addition to H, H should still correspond to a full binary tree (with one more node than before) that satisfies the heap property. The operation should take $O(\log n)$ time, where n is the number of objects in the heap.

Let's start with our running example:

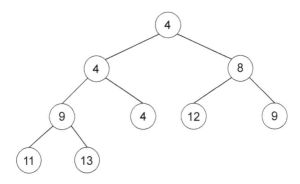

When a new object is inserted, the most obvious way to keep the tree full is to tack the new object onto the end of the array, or equivalently to the last level of the tree. (If the last level is already full, the object becomes the first at a new level.) As long as the implementation keeps track of the number n of objects (which is easy to do), this step takes constant time. For example, if we insert an object with key 7 into our running example, we obtain:

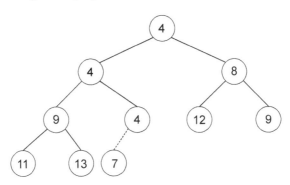

We have a full binary tree, but does the heap property hold? There's only one place it might fail—the one new parent-child pair (the 4 and the 7). In this case we got lucky, and the new pair doesn't violate the heap property. If our next insertion is an object with key 10, then again we get lucky and immediately obtain a valid heap:

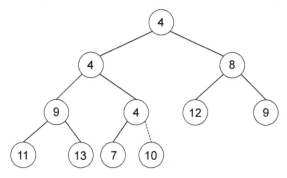

But suppose we now insert an object with key 5. After tacking it on at the end, our tree is:

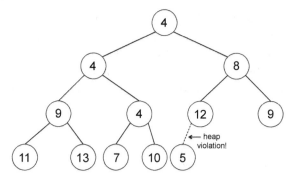

Now we have a problem: The new parent-child pair (the 12 and the 5) violates the heap property. What can we do about it? We can at least fix the problem locally by swapping the two nodes in the violating pair:

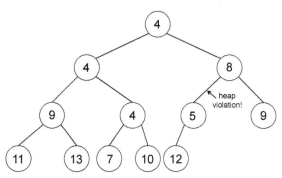

This fixes the violating parent-child pair. We're not out of the woods yet, however, as the heap violation has migrated upward to the 8 and the 5. So we do it again, and swap the nodes in the violating pair to obtain:

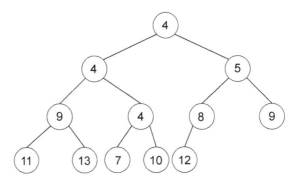

This explicitly fixes the violating pair. We've seen that such a swap has the potential to push the violation of the heap property upward, but here it doesn't happen—the 4 and 5 are already in the correct order. You might worry that a swap could also push the violation downward. But this also doesn't happen—the 8 and 12 are already in the correct order. With the heap property restored, the insertion is complete.

In general, the INSERT operation tacks the new object on to the end of the heap, and repeatedly swaps the nodes of a violating pair.[24] At all times, there is at most one violating parent-child pair—the pair in which the new object is the child.[25] Each swap pushes the violating parent-child pair up one level in the tree. This process cannot go on forever—if the new object makes it to the root, it has no parent and there can be no violating parent-child pair.

---

[24]This swapping subroutine goes by a number of names, including `Bubble-Up`, `Sift-Up`, `Heapify-Up`, and more.

[25]At no point are there any heap violations between the new object and its children. It has no children initially, and after a swap its children comprise the node it replaced (which has a larger key, as otherwise we wouldn't have swapped) and a previous child of that node (which, by the heap property, can have only a still larger key). Every parent-child pair not involving the new object appeared in the original heap, and hence does not violate the heap property. For instance, after two swaps in our example, the 8 and 12 are once again in a parent-child relationship, just like in the original heap.

> **INSERT**
>
> 1. Stick the new object at the end of the heap and increment the heap size.
>
> 2. Repeatedly swap the new object with its parent until the heap property is restored.

Because a heap is a full binary tree, it has $\approx \log_2 n$ levels, where n is the number of objects in the heap. The number of swaps is at most the number of levels, and only a constant amount of work is required per swap. We conclude that the worst-case running time of the INSERT operation is $O(\log n)$, as desired.

10.5.4   Implementing EXTRACTMIN in $O(\log n)$ Time

Recall the EXTRACTMIN operation:

> given a heap H, remove and return from H an object with the smallest key.

The root of the heap is guaranteed to be such an object. The challenge is to restore the full binary tree and heap properties after ripping out a heap's root.

We again keep the tree full in the most obvious way possible. Like INSERT in reverse, we know that the last node of the tree must go elsewhere. But where should it go? Because we're extracting the root anyway, let's overwrite the old root node with what used to be the last node. For example, starting from the heap

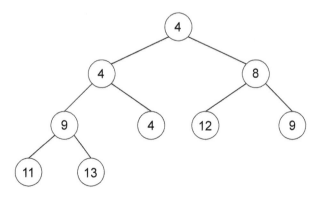

the resulting tree looks like

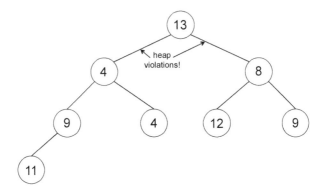

The good news is that we've restored the full binary tree property. The bad news is that the massive promotion granted to the object with key 13 has created two violating parent-child pairs (the 13 and 4 and the 13 and 8). Do we need two swaps to correct them?

The key idea is to swap the root node with the *smaller* of its two children:

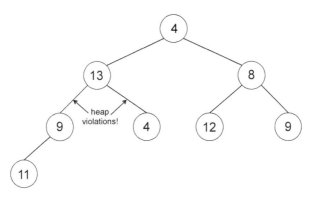

There are no longer any heap violations involving the root—the new root node is smaller than both the node it replaced (that's why we swapped) and its other child (as we swapped the smaller child).[26] The heap violations migrate downward, again involving the object with key 13 and its two (new) children. So we do it again, and swap the 13 with its smaller child:

---

[26]Swapping the 13 with the 8 would fail to vaccinate the left subtree from heap violations (with violating pair 8 and 4) while allowing the disease to spread to the right subtree (with violating pairs 13 and 12, and 13 and 9).

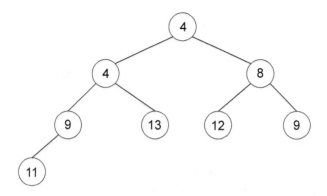

The heap property is restored at last, and now the extraction is complete.

In general, the EXTRACTMIN operation moves the last object of a heap to the root node (by overwriting the previous root), and repeatedly swaps this object with its smaller child.[27] At all times, there are at most two violating parent-child pairs—the two pairs in which the formerly-last object is the parent.[28] Because each swap pushes this object down one level in the tree, this process cannot go on forever—it stops once the new object belongs to the last level, if not earlier.

EXTRACTMIN

1. Overwrite the root with the last object x in the heap, and decrement the heap size.

2. Repeatedly swap x with its smaller child until the heap property is restored.

The number of swaps is at most the number of levels, and only a constant amount of work is required per swap. Because there are $\approx \log_2 n$ levels, we conclude that the worst-case running time of the EXTRACTMIN operation is $O(\log n)$, where n is the number of objects in the heap.

---

[27]This swapping subroutine is called, among other things, `Bubble-Down`.

[28]Every parent-child pair not involving this formerly-last object appeared in the original heap, and hence does not violate the heap property. There is also no violation involving this object and its parent—initially it had no parent, and subsequently it is swapped downward with objects that have smaller keys.

The Upshot

☆ There are many different data structures, each optimized for a different set of operations.

☆ The principle of parsimony recommends choosing the simplest data structure that supports all the operations required by your application.

☆ If your application requires fast minimum (or maximum) computations on an evolving set of objects, the heap is usually the data structure of choice.

☆ The two most important heap operations, INSERT and EXTRACTMIN, run in $O(\log n)$ time, where n is the number of objects.

☆ Heaps also support FINDMIN in $O(1)$ time, DELETE in $O(\log n)$ time, and HEAPIFY in $O(n)$ time.

☆ The HeapSort algorithm uses a heap to sort a length-n array in $O(n \log n)$ time.

☆ Heaps can be used to implement Dijkstra's shortest-path algorithm in $O((m + n) \log n)$ time, where m and n denote the number of edges and vertices of the graph, respectively.

☆ Heaps can be visualized as full binary trees but are implemented as arrays.

☆ The heap property states that the key of every object is less than or equal to the keys of its children.

☆ The INSERT and EXTRACTMIN operations are implemented by keeping the tree full in the

most obvious way possible and systematically
squashing any violations of the heap property.

Test Your Understanding

Problem 10.1 *(S)* Which of the following patterns in a computer
program suggests that a heap data structure could provide a significant
speed-up? (Check all that apply.)

a) Repeated lookups.

b) Repeated minimum computations.

c) Repeated maximum computations.

d) None of the other options.

Problem 10.2 Suppose you implement the functionality of a priority
queue (that is, INSERT and EXTRACTMIN) using an array sorted from
largest to smallest. What is the worst-case running time of INSERT
and EXTRACTMIN, respectively? Assume you have a large enough
array to accommodate all your insertions.

a) $\Theta(1)$ and $\Theta(n)$

b) $\Theta(n)$ and $\Theta(1)$

c) $\Theta(\log n)$ and $\Theta(1)$

d) $\Theta(n)$ and $\Theta(n)$

Problem 10.3 Suppose you implement the functionality of a priority
queue (that is, INSERT and EXTRACTMIN) using an *unsorted* array.
What is the worst-case running time of INSERT and EXTRACTMIN,
respectively? Assume you have a large enough array to accommodate
all your insertions.

a) $\Theta(1)$ and $\Theta(n)$

b) $\Theta(n)$ and $\Theta(1)$

c) $\Theta(1)$ and $\Theta(\log n)$

d) $\Theta(n)$ and $\Theta(n)$

Problem 10.4 *(S)* You are given a heap with n objects. Which of the following tasks can you solve using $O(1)$ INSERT and EXTRACTMIN operations and $O(1)$ additional work? (Choose all that apply.)

a) Find the object stored in the heap with the fifth-smallest key.

b) Find the object stored in the heap with the maximum key.

c) Find the object stored in the heap with the median key.

d) None of the above.

Challenge Problems

Problem 10.5 *(S)* Continuing Problem 9.7, show how to modify the heap-based implementation of Dijkstra's algorithm to compute, for each vertex $v \in V$, the smallest bottleneck of an s-v path. Your algorithm should run in $O((m + n) \log n)$ time, where m and n denote the number of edges and vertices, respectively.

Problem 10.6 (Difficult.) We can do better. Suppose now the graph is undirected. Give a linear-time (that is, $O(m + n)$-time) algorithm to compute a minimum-bottleneck path between two given vertices.

[Hint: A linear-time algorithm from *Part 1* will come in handy. In the recursion, aim to cut the input size in half in linear time.]

Problem 10.7 (Difficult.) What if the graph is directed? Can you compute a minimum-bottleneck path between two given vertices in less than $O((m + n) \log n)$ time?[29]

---

[29]For a deep dive on this problem, see the paper "Algorithms for Two Bottleneck Optimization Problems," by Harold N. Gabow and Robert E. Tarjan (*Journal of Algorithms*, 1988).

Programming Problems

Problem 10.8 Implement in your favorite programming language the heap-based version of the `Dijkstra` algorithm from Section 10.4, and use it to solve the single-source shortest path problem in different directed graphs. With this heap-based implementation, what's the size of the largest problem you can solve in five minutes or less? (See `www.algorithmsilluminated.org` for test cases and challenge data sets.)

[Hint: This requires the DELETE operation, which may force you to implement a customized heap data structure from scratch. To delete an object from a heap at a given position, follow the high-level approach of INSERT and EXTRACTMIN, using `Bubble-Up` or `Bubble-Down` as needed to squash violations of the heap property. You will also need to keep track of which vertex is in which position of your heap, perhaps by using a hash table (Chapter 12).]

Chapter 11

Search Trees

A *search tree*, like a heap, is a data structure for storing an evolving set of objects associated with keys (and possibly lots of other data). It maintains a total ordering over the stored objects, and can support a richer set of operations than a heap, at the expense of increased space and, for some operations, somewhat slower running times. We'll start with the "what" (that is, supported operations) before proceeding to the "why" (applications) and the "how" (optional implementation details).

11.1 Sorted Arrays

A good way to think about a search tree is as a dynamic version of a sorted array—it can do everything a sorted array can do, while also accommodating fast insertions and deletions.

11.1.1 Sorted Arrays: Supported Operations

You can do a lot of things with a sorted array.

Sorted Arrays: Supported Operations

SEARCH: for a key k, return a pointer to an object in the data structure with key k (or report that no such object exists).

MIN (MAX): return a pointer to the object in the data structure with the smallest (respectively, largest) key.

PREDECESSOR (SUCCESSOR): given a pointer to an object in the data structure, return a pointer to the object with

---

the next-smallest (respectively, next-largest) key. If the given object has the minimum (respectively, maximum) key, report "none."

OUTPUTSORTED: output the objects in the data structure one by one in order of their keys.

SELECT: given a number i, between 1 and the number of objects, return a pointer to the object in the data structure with the ith-smallest key.

RANK: given a key k, return the number of objects in the data structure with key at most k.

Let's review how to implement each of these operations, with the following running example:

| 3 | 6 | 10 | 11 | 17 | 23 | 30 | 36 |

- The SEARCH operation uses binary search: First check if the object in the middle position of the array has the desired key. If so, return it. If not, recurse either on the left half (if the middle object's key is too large) or on the right half (if it's too small).[1] For example, to search the array above for the key 8, binary search will: examine the fourth object (with key 11); recurse on the left half (the objects with keys 3, 6, and 10); check the second object (with key 6); recurse on the right half of the remaining array (the object with key 10); conclude that the rightful position for an object with key 8 would be between the second and third objects; and report "none." As each recursive call cuts the array size by a factor of 2, there are at most $\log_2 n$ recursive calls, where n is the length of the array. Because each recursive call does a constant amount of work, the operation runs in $O(\log n)$ time.

---

[1] Readers of at least a certain age should be reminded of searching for a phone number in a phone book. If you haven't walked through the code of this algorithm before, look it up in your favorite introductory programming book or tutorial.

- MIN and MAX are easy to implement in $O(1)$ time: Return a pointer to the first or last object in the array, respectively.

- To implement PREDECESSOR or SUCCESSOR, use the SEARCH operation to recover the position of the given object in the sorted array, and return the object in the previous or next position, respectively. These operations are as fast as SEARCH—running in $O(\log n)$ time, where n is the length of the array.

- The OUTPUTSORTED operation is trivial to implement in linear time with a sorted array: Perform a single front-to-back pass over the array, outputting each object in turn.

- SELECT is easy to implement in constant time: Given an index i, return the object in the ith position of the array.

- The RANK operation, which is like an inverse of SELECT, can be implemented along the same lines as SEARCH: If binary search finds an object with key k in the ith position of the array, or if it discovers that k is in between the keys of the objects in the ith and $(i + 1)$th positions, the correct answer is i.[2]

Summarizing, here's the final scorecard for sorted arrays:

Operation	Running time
SEARCH	$O(\log n)$
MIN	$O(1)$
MAX	$O(1)$
PREDECESSOR	$O(\log n)$
SUCCESSOR	$O(\log n)$
OUTPUTSORTED	$O(n)$
SELECT	$O(1)$
RANK	$O(\log n)$

Table 11.1: Sorted arrays: supported operations and their running times, where n denotes the current number of objects stored in the array.

---

[2]This description assumes, for simplicity, that there are no duplicate keys. What changes are necessary to accommodate multiple objects with the same key?

11.1.2   Unsupported Operations

Could you really ask for anything more? With a *static* data set that does not change over time, this is an impressive list of supported operations. Many real-world applications are *dynamic*, however, with the set of relevant objects evolving over time. For example, employees come and go, and the data structure that stores their records should stay up to date. For this reason, we also care about insertions and deletions.

Sorted Arrays: Unsupported Operations

INSERT: given a new object x, add x to the data structure.

DELETE: for a key k, delete an object with key k from the data structure, if one exists.[3]

These two operations aren't impossible to implement with a sorted array, but they're painfully slow—inserting or deleting an element while maintaining the sorted array property requires linear time in the worst case. Is there an alternative data structure that replicates all the functionality of a sorted array, while matching the logarithmic-time performance of a heap for the INSERT and DELETE operations?

11.2   Search Trees: Supported Operations

The raison d'être of a search tree is to support all the operations that a sorted array supports, plus insertions and deletions. All the operations except OUTPUTSORTED run in $O(\log n)$ time, where n is the number of objects in the search tree. The OUTPUTSORTED operation runs in $O(n)$ time, and this is as good as it gets (since it must output n objects).

Here's the scorecard for search trees, with a comparison to sorted arrays:

---

[3]The eagle-eyed reader may have noticed that this specification of the DELETE operation (which takes a key as input) is different from the one for heaps (which takes a pointer to an object as input). This is because heaps do not support fast search. In a sorted array (as well as in search trees and hash tables), it's easy to recover a pointer to an object given its key (via SEARCH).

Operation	Sorted Array	Balanced Search Tree
SEARCH	$O(\log n)$	$O(\log n)$
MIN	$O(1)$	$O(\log n)$
MAX	$O(1)$	$O(\log n)$
PREDECESSOR	$O(\log n)$	$O(\log n)$
SUCCESSOR	$O(\log n)$	$O(\log n)$
OUTPUTSORTED	$O(n)$	$O(n)$
SELECT	$O(1)$	$O(\log n)$
RANK	$O(\log n)$	$O(\log n)$
INSERT	$O(n)$	$O(\log n)$
DELETE	$O(n)$	$O(\log n)$

Table 11.2: Balanced search trees vs. sorted arrays: supported operations and their running times, where n denotes the current number of objects stored in the data structure.

An important caveat: The running times in Table 11.2 are achieved by a *balanced* search tree, which is a more sophisticated version of the standard binary search tree described in Section 11.3. These running times are *not* guaranteed by an unbalanced search tree.[4]

When to Use a Balanced Search Tree

If your application requires maintaining an ordered representation of a dynamically changing set of objects, the balanced search tree (or a data structure based on one[5]) is usually the data structure of choice.[6]

---

[4] A preview of Sections 11.3 and 11.4: In general, search tree operations run in time proportional to the *height* of the tree, meaning the longest path from the tree's root to one of its leaves. In a binary tree with n nodes, the height can be anywhere from $\approx \log_2 n$ (if the tree is perfectly balanced) to $n - 1$ (if the nodes form a single chain). Balanced search trees do a modest amount of extra work to ensure that the height is always $O(\log n)$; this height guarantee then leads to the running time bounds in Table 11.2.

[5] For example, the `TreeMap` class in Java and the `map` class template in the C++ Standard Template Library are built on top of balanced search trees.

[6] One good place to see balanced search trees in the wild is in the Linux kernel. For example, they are used to manage the scheduling of processes, and to keep track of the virtual memory footprint of each process.

Remember the principle of parsimony: Choose the simplest data structure that supports all the operations required by your application. If you need to maintain only an ordered representation of a static data set (with no insertions or deletions), use a sorted array instead of a balanced search tree; the latter would be overkill. If your data set is dynamic but you care only about fast minimum (or maximum) operations, use a heap instead of a balanced search tree. These simpler data structures do less than a balanced search tree, but what they do, they do better—faster (by a constant or logarithmic factor) and with less space (by a constant factor).[7]

*11.3   Implementation Details

This section provides a high-level description of a typical implementation of a (not necessarily balanced) binary search tree. Section 11.4 touches on some of the extra ideas needed for balanced search trees.

11.3.1   The Search Tree Property

In a binary search tree, every node corresponds to an object (with a key) and has three pointers associated with it: a parent pointer, a left child pointer, and a right child pointer. Any of these pointers can be null, indicating the absence of a parent or child. The left subtree of a node x comprises the nodes reachable from x via its left child pointer, and similarly for the right subtree. The defining *search tree property* is:[8]

The Search Tree Property

1. For every object x, objects in x's left subtree have keys smaller than that of x.

2. For every object x, objects in x's right subtree have keys larger than that of x.[9]

---

[7]Chapter 12 covers hash tables, which do still less; but what they do, they do even better (constant time, for all practical purposes).

[8]We refer to nodes and the corresponding objects interchangeably.

[9]This assumes no two objects have the same key. To accommodate duplicate keys, change the "smaller than" in the first condition to "smaller than or equal to."

The search tree property imposes a requirement for *every* node of a search tree, not just for the root:

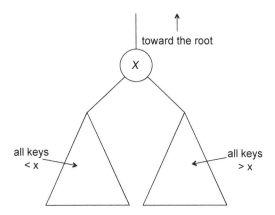

For example, here's a search tree containing objects with the keys $\{1, 2, 3, 4, 5\}$, and a table listing the destinations of the three pointers at each node:

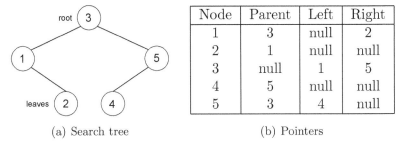

Node	Parent	Left	Right
1	3	null	2
2	1	null	null
3	null	1	5
4	5	null	null
5	3	4	null

(a) Search tree   (b) Pointers

Figure 11.1: A search tree and its corresponding parent and child pointers.

Binary search trees and heaps differ in several ways. Heaps can be thought of as trees, but they are implemented as arrays, with no explicit pointers between objects. A search tree explicitly stores three pointers per object, and hence uses more space (by a constant factor). Heaps don't need explicit pointers because they always correspond to full binary trees, while binary search trees can have an arbitrary structure.

Search trees have a different purpose than heaps. For this reason, the search tree property is incomparable to the heap property. Heaps

are optimized for fast minimum computations, and the heap property—
that a child's key is only bigger than its parent's key—makes the
minimum-key object easy to find (it's the root). Search trees are
optimized for—wait for it—search, and the search tree property is
defined accordingly. For example, if you are searching for an object
with the key 23 in a search tree and the root's key is 17, you know
that the object can reside only in the root's right subtree, and can
discard the objects in the left subtree from further consideration. This
should remind you of binary search, as befits a data structure whose
raison d'être is to simulate a dynamically changing sorted array.

11.3.2   The Height of a Search Tree

Many different search trees exist for a given set of keys. Here's a
second search tree containing objects with the keys $\{1, 2, 3, 4, 5\}$:

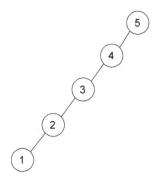

Both conditions in the search tree property hold, the second one
vacuously (as there are no non-empty right subtrees).

The *height* of a tree is defined as the length of a longest path from
its root to a leaf.[10] Different search trees containing identical sets of
objects can have different heights, as in our first two examples (which
have heights 2 and 4, respectively). In general, a binary search tree
containing n objects can have a height anywhere from

$$\underbrace{\approx \log_2 n}_{\substack{\text{perfectly balanced binary tree} \\ \text{(best-case scenario)}}} \qquad \text{to} \qquad \underbrace{n - 1.}_{\substack{\text{chain, as above} \\ \text{(worst-case scenario)}}}$$

The rest of this section outlines how to implement all the operations
of a binary search tree in time proportional to the tree's height (save

---

[10] Also known as the *depth* of the tree.

OUTPUTSORTED, which runs in time linear in n). For the refinements of binary search trees that are guaranteed to have height $O(\log n)$ (see Section 11.4), this leads to the logarithmic running times reported in the scorecard in Table 11.2.

11.3.3 Implementing SEARCH in $O(height)$ Time

Let's begin with the SEARCH operation:

> for a key k, return a pointer to an object in the data structure with key k (or report that no such object exists).

The search tree property tells you exactly where to look for an object with key k. If k is less than (respectively, greater than) the root's key, such an object must reside in the root's left subtree (respectively, right tree). To search, follow your nose: Start at the root and repeatedly go left or right (as appropriate) until you find the desired object (a successful search) or encounter a null pointer (an unsuccessful search).

For example, suppose we search for an object with key 2 in our first binary search tree:

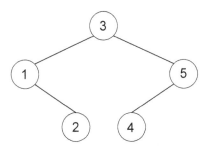

Because the root's key (3) is too big, the first step traverses the left child pointer. Because the next node's key is too small (1), the second step traverses the right child pointer, arriving at the desired object. If we search for an object with key 6, the search traverses the root's right child pointer (as the root's key is too small). Because the next node's key (5) is also too small, the search tries to follow another right child pointer, encounters a null pointer, and halts the search (unsuccessfully).

SEARCH

1. Start at the root node.

2. Repeatedly traverse left and right child pointers, as appropriate (left if k is less than the current node's key, right if k is bigger).

3. Return a pointer to an object with key k (if found) or "none" (upon reaching a null pointer).

The running time is proportional to the number of pointers followed, which is at most the height of the search tree (plus 1, if you count the final null pointer of an unsuccessful search).

11.3.4   Implementing MIN and MAX in $O(height)$ Time

The search tree property makes it easy to implement the MIN and MAX operations.

MIN (MAX): return a pointer to the object in the data structure with the smallest (respectively, largest) key.

Keys in the left subtree of the root can only be smaller than the root's key, and keys in the right subtree can only be larger. If the left subtree is empty, the root must be the minimum. Otherwise, the minimum of the left subtree is also the minimum of the entire tree. This suggests following the root's left child pointer and repeating the process.

For example, in the search trees we considered earlier:

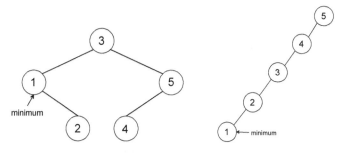

repeatedly following left child pointers leads to the object with the minimum key.

MIN (MAX)

1. Start at the root node.

2. Traverse left child pointers (right child pointers) as long as possible, until encountering a null pointer.

3. Return a pointer to the last object visited.

The running time is proportional to the number of pointers followed, which is $O(height)$.

11.3.5   Implementing PREDECESSOR in $O(height)$ Time

Next is the PREDECESSOR operation; the implementation of the SUCCESSOR operation is analogous.

> PREDECESSOR: given a pointer to an object in the data structure, return a pointer to the object with the next-smallest key. (If the object has the minimum key, report "none.")

Given an object x, where could x's predecessor reside? Not in x's right subtree, where all the keys are larger than x's key (by the search tree property). Our running example

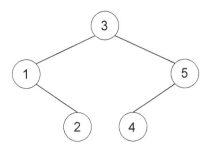

illustrates two cases. The predecessor might appear in the left subtree (as for the nodes with keys 3 and 5), or it could be an ancestor farther up in the tree (as for the nodes with keys 2 and 4).

The general pattern is: If an object x's left subtree is non-empty, this subtree's maximum element is x's predecessor[11]; otherwise, x's predecessor is the closest ancestor of x that has a smaller key than x. Equivalently, tracing parent pointers upward from x, it is the destination of the first left turn.[12] For example, in the search tree above, tracing parent pointers upward from the node with key 4 first takes a right turn (leading to a node with the bigger key 5) and then takes a left turn, arriving at the correct predecessor (3). If x has an empty left subtree and no left turns above it, then it is the minimum in the search tree and has no predecessor (like the node with key 1 in the search tree above).

PREDECESSOR

1. If x's left subtree is non-empty, return the result of MAX applied to this subtree.

2. Otherwise, traverse parent pointers upward toward the root. If the traversal visits consecutive nodes y and z with y a right child of z, return a pointer to z.

3. Otherwise, report "none."

The running time is proportional to the number of pointers followed, which in all cases is $O(height)$.

11.3.6   Implementing OUTPUTSORTED in $O(n)$ Time

Recall the OUTPUTSORTED operation:

> OUTPUTSORTED: output the objects in the data structure one by one in order of their keys.

A lazy way to implement this operation is to first use the MIN operation to output the object with the minimum key, and then repeatedly

---

[11]Among the keys less than x's, the ones in x's left subtree are the closest to x (as you should check). Among the keys in this subtree, the maximum is the closest to x.

[12]Right turns can lead only to nodes with larger keys, which cannot be x's predecessor. The search tree property also implies that neither more distant ancestors nor non-ancestors can be x's predecessor (as you should check).

invoke the SUCCESSOR operation to output the rest of the objects in order. A better method is to use what's called an *in-order traversal* of the search tree, which recursively processes the root's left subtree, then the root, and then the root's right subtree. This idea meshes perfectly with the search tree property, which implies that OUTPUT-SORTED should first output the objects in the root's left subtree in order, followed by the object at the root, followed by the objects in the root's right subtree in order.

OUTPUTSORTED

1. Recursively call OUTPUTSORTED on the root's left subtree.

2. Output the object at the root.

3. Recursively call OUTPUTSORTED on the root's right subtree.

For a tree containing n objects, the operation performs n recursive calls (one initiated at each node) and does a constant amount of work in each, for a total running time of $O(n)$.

11.3.7   Implementing INSERT in $O(height)$ Time

None of the operations discussed so far modify the given search tree, so they run no risk of screwing up the crucial search tree property. Our next two operations—INSERT and DELETE—make changes to the tree, and must take care to preserve the search tree property.

INSERT: given a new object x, add x to the data structure.

The INSERT operation piggybacks on SEARCH. An unsuccessful search for an object with key k locates where such an object would have appeared. This is the appropriate place to stick a new object with key k (rewiring the old null pointer). In our running example, the correct location for a new object with key 6 is the spot where our unsuccessful search concluded:

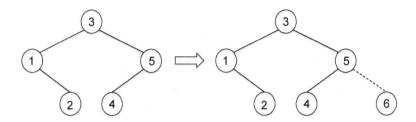

What if there is already an object with key k in the tree? If you want to avoid duplicate keys, the insertion can be ignored. Otherwise, the search follows the left child of the existing object with key k, pushing onward until a null pointer is encountered.

INSERT

1. Start at the root node.

2. Repeatedly traverse left and right child pointers, as appropriate (left if k is at most the current node's key, right if it's bigger), until a null pointer is encountered.

3. Replace the null pointer with one to the new object. Set the new node's parent pointer to its parent, and its child pointers to null.

The operation preserves the search tree property because it places the new object where it should have been.[13] The running time is the same as for SEARCH, which is $O(height)$.

11.3.8   Implementing DELETE in $O(height)$ Time

In most data structures, the DELETE operation is the toughest one to get right. Search trees are no exception.

DELETE: for a key k, delete an object with key k from the search tree, if one exists.

---

[13]More formally, let x denote the newly inserted object and consider an existing object y. If x is not a member of the subtree rooted at y, then it cannot interfere with the search tree property at y. If it is a member of the subtree rooted at y, then y was one of the nodes visited during the unsuccessful search for x. The keys of x and y were explicitly compared in this search, with x placed in y's left subtree if and only if its key is no larger than y's.

The main challenge is to repair a tree after a node removal so that
the search tree property is restored.

The first step is to invoke SEARCH to locate an object x with
key k. (If there is no such object, DELETE has nothing to do.) There
are three cases, depending on whether x has 0, 1, or 2 children. If x
is a leaf, it can be deleted without harm. For example, if we delete
the node with key 2 from our favorite search tree:

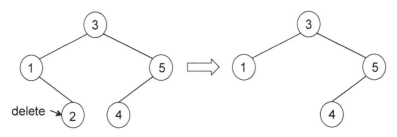

For every remaining node y, the nodes in y's subtrees are the same
as before, except possibly with x removed; the search tree property
continues to hold.

When x has one child y, we can splice it out. Deleting x leaves y
without a parent and x's old parent z without one of its children. The
obvious fix is to let y assume x's previous position (as z's child).[14]
For example, if we delete the node with key 5 from our favorite search
tree:

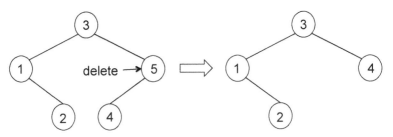

By the same reasoning as in the first case, the search property is
preserved.

The hard case is when x has two children. Deleting x leaves *two*
nodes without a parent, and it's not clear where to put them. In our
running example, it's not obvious how to repair the tree after deleting
its root.

---

[14]Insert your favorite nerdy Shakespeare joke here...

The key trick is to reduce the hard case to one of the easy ones. First, use the PREDECESSOR operation to compute the predecessor y of x.[15] Because x has two children, its predecessor is the object in its (non-empty!) left subtree with the maximum key (see Section 11.3.5). Since the maximum is computed by following right child pointers as long as possible (see Section 11.3.4), y cannot have a right child; it might or might not have a left child.

Here's a crazy idea: *Swap x and y!* In our running example, with the root node acting as x:

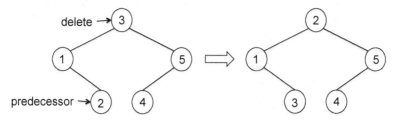

This crazy idea looks like a bad one, as we've now violated the search tree property (with the node with key 3 in the left subtree of the node with key 2). But every violation of the search tree property involves the node x, which we're going to delete anyway.[16] Because x now occupies y's previous position, it no longer has a right child. Deleting x from its new position falls into one of the two easy cases: We delete it if it also has no left child, and splice it out if it does have a left child. Either way, with x out of the picture, the search tree property is restored. Back to our running example:

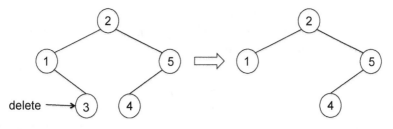

---

[15]The successor also works fine, if you prefer.

[16]For every node z other than y, the only possible new node in z's subtree is x. Meanwhile y, as x's immediate predecessor in the sorted ordering of all keys, has a key larger than those in x's old left subtree and greater than those in x's old right subtree. Thus, the search tree condition holds for y in its new position, except with respect to x.

DELETE

1. Use SEARCH to locate an object x with key k. (If no such object exists, halt.)

2. If x has no children, delete x by setting the appropriate child pointer of x's parent to null. (If x was the root, the new tree is empty.)

3. If x has one child, splice x out by rewiring the appropriate child pointer of x's parent to x's child, and the parent pointer of x's child to x's parent. (If x was the root, its child becomes the new root.)

4. Otherwise, swap x with the object in its left subtree that has the biggest key, and delete x from its new position (where it has at most one child).

The operation performs a constant amount of work in addition to one SEARCH and one PREDECESSOR operation, so it runs in $O(height)$ time.

11.3.9   Augmented Search Trees for SELECT

Finally, the SELECT operation:

SELECT: given a number i, between 1 and the number of objects, return a pointer to the object in the data structure with the ith-smallest key.

To get SELECT to run quickly, we'll *augment* the search tree by having each node keep track of information *about the structure of the tree itself*, and not just about an object.[17] Search trees can be augmented in many ways; here, we'll store at each node x an integer $size(x)$ indicating the number of nodes in the subtree rooted at x (including x itself). In our running example

---

[17]This idea can also be used to implement the RANK operation in $O(height)$ time (as you should check).

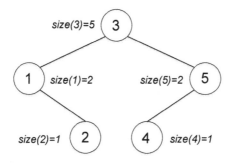

we have $size(1) = 2$, $size(2) = 1$, $size(3) = 5$, $size(4) = 1$, and $size(5) = 2$.

Quiz 11.1

Suppose the node x in a search tree has children y and z. What is the relationship between $size(x)$, $size(y)$, and $size(z)$?

a) $size(x) = \max\{size(y), size(z)\} + 1$

b) $size(x) = size(y) + size(z)$

c) $size(x) = size(y) + size(z) + 1$

d) There is no general relationship.

(See Section 11.3.10 for the solution and discussion.)

How is this additional information helpful? Imagine you're looking for the object with the 17th-smallest key (i.e., $i = 17$) in a search tree with 100 objects. Starting at the root, you can compute in constant time the sizes of its left and right subtrees. By the search tree property, every key in the left subtree is less than those at the root and in the right subtree. If the population of the left subtree is 25, these are the 25 smallest keys in the tree, including the 17th-smallest key. If its population is only 12, the right subtree contains all but the 13 smallest keys, and the 17th-smallest key is the 4th-smallest among its 87 keys. Either way, we can call SELECT recursively to locate the desired object.

SELECT

1. Start at the root and let j be the size of its left subtree. (If it has no left child pointer, then $j = 0$.)

2. If $i = j + 1$, return a pointer to the root.

3. If $i < j + 1$, recursively compute the ith-smallest key in the left subtree.

4. If $i > j + 1$, recursively compute the $(i - j - 1)$th smallest key in the right subtree.[18]

Because each node of the search tree stores the size of its subtree, each recursive call performs only a constant amount of work. Each recursive call proceeds further downward in the tree, so the total amount of work is $O(height)$.

Paying the piper. We still have to pay the piper. We've added and exploited metadata to the search tree, and every operation that modifies the tree must take care to keep this information up to date, in addition to preserving the search tree property. You should think through how to re-implement the INSERT and DELETE operations, still running in $O(height)$ time, so that all the subtree sizes remain accurate.[19]

11.3.10   Solution to Quiz 11.1

Correct answer: (c). Every node in the subtree rooted at x is either x itself, or a node in x's left subtree, or a node in x's right subtree. We therefore have

$$size(x) = \underbrace{size(y)}_{\text{nodes in left subtree}} + \underbrace{size(z)}_{\text{nodes in right subtree}} + \underbrace{1}_{x}.$$

---

[18]The structure of the recursion might remind you of our selection algorithms in Chapter 6 of *Part 1*, with the root node playing the role of the pivot element.

[19]For example, for the INSERT operation, increment the subtree size for every node on the path between the root and the newly inserted object.

*11.4   Balanced Search Trees

11.4.1   Working Harder for Better Balance

The running time of every binary search tree operation (save OUT-PUTSORTED) is proportional to the tree's height, which can range anywhere from the best-case scenario of $\approx \log_2 n$ (for a perfectly balanced tree) to the worst-case scenario of $n - 1$ (for a chain), where n is the number of objects in the tree. Badly unbalanced search trees really can occur, for example when objects are inserted in sorted or reverse sorted order:

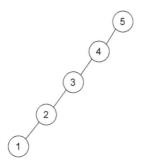

The difference between a logarithmic and a linear running time is huge, so it's a win to work a little harder in INSERT and DELETE—still $O(height)$ time, but with a larger constant factor—to guarantee that the tree's height is always $O(\log n)$.

Several different types of balanced search trees guarantee $O(\log n)$ height and, hence, achieve the operation running times stated in the scorecard in Table 11.2.[20] The devil is in the implementation details, and they can get pretty tricky for balanced search trees. Happily, implementations are readily available and it's unlikely that you'll ever need to code up your own version from scratch. I encourage readers interested in what's under the hood of a balanced search tree to check out a textbook treatment or explore the open-source implementations and visualization demos that are freely available online.[21] To whet

---

[20]Popular ones include red-black trees, 2-3 trees, AVL trees, splay trees, and B and B+ trees.

[21]Standard textbook treatments include Chapter 13 of *Introduction to Algorithms (Third Edition)*, by Thomas H. Cormen, Charles E. Leiserson, Ronald L. Rivest, and Clifford Stein (MIT Press, 2009); and Section 3.3 of *Algorithms (Fourth Edition)*, by Robert Sedgewick and Kevin Wayne (Addison-Wesley, 2011).

your appetite for further study, let's conclude the chapter with one of the most ubiquitous ideas in balanced search tree implementations.

11.4.2   Rotations

All the most common implementations of balanced search trees use *rotations*, a constant-time operation that performs a modest amount of local rebalancing while preserving the search tree property. For example, we could imagine transforming the chain of five objects above into a more civilized search tree by composing two local rebalancing operations:

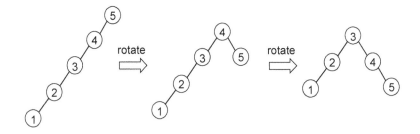

A rotation takes a parent-child pair and reverses their relationship (Figure 11.2). A *right rotation* applies when the child y is the left child of its parent x (and so y has a smaller key than x); after the rotation, x is the right child of y. When y is the right child of x, a *left rotation* makes x the left child of y.

The search tree property dictates the remaining details. For example, consider a left rotation, with y the right child of x. The search tree property implies that x's key is less than y's; that all the keys in x's left subtree ("A" in Figure 11.2) are less than that of x (and y); that all the keys in y's right subtree ("C" in Figure 11.2) are greater than that of y (and x); and that all the keys in y's left subtree ("B" in Figure 11.2) are between those of x and y. After the rotation, y inherits x's old parent and has x as its new left child. There's a unique way to put all the pieces back together while preserving the search tree property, so let's just follow our nose.

There are three free slots for the subtrees A, B, and C: y's right child pointer and both child pointers of x. The search tree property

---

See also the bonus videos at **www.algorithmsilluminated.org** for the basics of red-black trees.

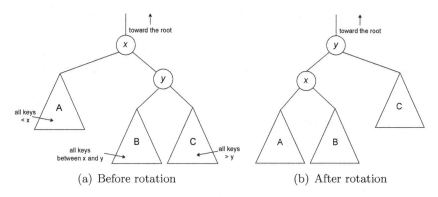

(a) Before rotation   (b) After rotation

Figure 11.2: A left rotation in action.

forces us to stick the smallest subtree (A) as x's left child, and the largest subtree (C) as y's right child. This leaves one slot for subtree B (x's right child pointer), and fortunately the search tree property works out: All the subtree's keys are wedged between those of x and y, and the subtree winds up in y's left subtree (where it needs to be) and x's right subtree (ditto).

A right rotation is then a left rotation in reverse (Figure 11.3).

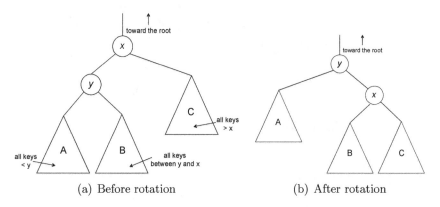

(a) Before rotation   (b) After rotation

Figure 11.3: A right rotation in action.

Because a rotation merely rewires a few pointers, it can be implemented with a constant number of operations. By construction, it preserves the search tree property.

The operations that modify the search tree—INSERT and DELETE—

are the ones that must employ rotations. Without rotations, such
an operation might render the tree a little more unbalanced. Since a
single insertion or deletion can wreak only so much havoc, it should
be plausible that a small—constant or perhaps logarithmic—number
of rotations can correct any newly created imbalance. This is exactly what the aforementioned balanced search tree implementations
do. The extra work from rotations adds $O(\log n)$ overhead to the
INSERT and DELETE operations, leaving their overall running times
at $O(\log n)$.

The Upshot

☆ If your application requires maintaining a totally ordered representation of an evolving set
of objects, the balanced search tree is usually
the data structure of choice.

☆ Balanced search trees support the operations
SEARCH, MIN, MAX, PREDECESSOR, SUCCES-
SOR, SELECT, RANK, INSERT, and DELETE in
$O(\log n)$ time, where n is the number of objects.

☆ A binary search tree has one node per object,
each with a parent pointer, a left child pointer,
and a right child pointer.

☆ The search tree property states that, at every
node x of the tree, the keys in x's left subtree
are smaller than x's key, and the keys in x's
right subtree are larger than x's key.

☆ The *height* of a search tree is the length of a
longest path from its root to a leaf. A binary
search tree with n objects can have height anywhere from $\approx \log_2 n$ to $n - 1$.

☆ In a basic binary search tree, all the supported operations above can be implemented in
$O(\mathit{height})$ time. (For SELECT and RANK, after

augmenting the tree to maintain subtree sizes at each node.)

☆ Balanced binary search trees do extra work in the INSERT and DELETE operations—still $O(height)$ time, but with a larger constant factor—to guarantee that the tree's height is always $O(\log n)$.

Test Your Understanding

Problem 11.1 *(S)* Which of the following statements are true? (Check all that apply.)

a) The height of a binary search tree with n nodes cannot be smaller than $\Theta(\log n)$.

b) All the operations supported by a binary search tree (except OUTPUTSORTED) run in $O(\log n)$ time.

c) The heap property is a special case of the search tree property.

d) Balanced binary search trees are always preferable to sorted arrays.

Problem 11.2 You are given a binary tree with n nodes (via a pointer to its root). Each node of the tree has a *size* field, as in Section 11.3.9, but these fields have not been filled in yet. How much time is necessary and sufficient to compute the correct value for all the *size* fields?

a) $\Theta(height)$

b) $\Theta(n)$

c) $\Theta(n \log n)$

d) $\Theta(n^2)$

Programming Problems

Problem 11.3 This problem uses the median maintenance problem from Section 10.3.3 to explore the relative performance of heaps and search trees.

a) Implement in your favorite programming language the heap-based solution in Section 10.3.3 to the median maintenance problem.

b) Implement a solution to the problem that uses a single search tree and its INSERT and SELECT operations.

Which implementation is faster?

You can use existing implementations of heaps and search trees, or you can implement your own from scratch. (See www. algorithmsilluminated.org for test cases and challenge data sets.)

Chapter 12

Hash Tables and Bloom Filters

We conclude with an incredibly useful and ubiquitous data structure known as a *hash table* (or *hash map*). Hash tables, like heaps and search trees, maintain an evolving set of objects associated with keys (and possibly lots of other data). Unlike heaps and search trees, they maintain no ordering information whatsoever. The raison d'être of a hash table is to facilitate super-fast searches, which are also called *lookups* in this context. A hash table can tell you what's there and what's not, and can do it really, really quickly (much faster than a heap or search tree). As usual, we'll start with the supported operations (Section 12.1) before proceeding to applications (Section 12.2) and some optional implementation details (Sections 12.3 and 12.4). Sections 12.5 and 12.6 cover *bloom filters*, close cousins of hash tables that use less space at the expense of occasional errors.

12.1 Supported Operations

The raison d'être of a hash table is to keep track of an evolving set of objects with keys while supporting fast lookups (by key), so that it's easy to check what's there and what's not. For example, if your company manages an ecommerce site, you might use one hash table to keep track of employees (perhaps with names as keys), another one to store past transactions (with transaction IDs as keys), and a third to remember the visitors to your site (with IP addresses as keys).

Conceptually, you can think of a hash table as an array. One thing that arrays are good for is immediate random access. Wondering what's in position number 17 of an array? Just access that position directly, in constant time. Want to change the contents in position 23? Again, easy in constant time.

Suppose you want a data structure for remembering your friends' phone numbers. If you're lucky, all your friends had unusually unimaginative parents who named their kids after positive integers, say between 1 and 10000. In this case, you can store phone numbers in a length-10000 array (which is not that big). If your best friend is named 173, store their phone number in position 173 of the array. To forget about your ex-friend 548, overwrite position 548 with a default value. This array-based solution works well, even if your friends change over time—the space requirements are modest and insertions, deletions, and lookups run in constant time.

Probably your friends have more interesting but less convenient names, like Alice, Bob, Carol, and so on. Can we still use an array-based solution? In principle, you could maintain an array with entries indexed by every possible name you might ever see (with at most, say, 25 letters). To look up Alice's phone number, you can then look in the "Alice" position of the array (Figure 12.1).

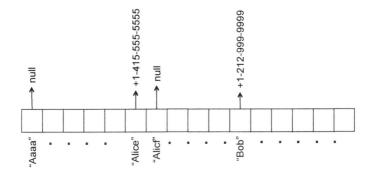

Figure 12.1: In principle, you could store your friends' phone numbers in an array indexed by strings with at most 25 characters.

Quiz 12.1

How many length-25 character strings are there? (Choose the strongest true statement.)

a) More than the number of hairs on your head.

b) More than the number of Web pages in existence.

c) More than the total amount of storage available on Earth (in bits).

> d) More than the number of atoms in the universe.
>
> (See Section 12.1.1 for the solution and discussion.)

The point of Quiz 12.1 is that the array needed for this solution is WAY TOO BIG. Is there an alternative data structure that replicates all the functionality of an array, with constant-time insertions, deletions, and lookups, and that also uses space proportional to the number of objects stored? A hash table is exactly such a data structure.

Hash Tables: Supported Operations

LOOKUP (a.k.a. SEARCH): for a key k, return a pointer to an object in the hash table with key k (or report that no such object exists).

INSERT: given a new object x, add x to the hash table.

DELETE: for a key k, delete an object with key k from the hash table, if one exists.

In a hash table, all these operations typically run in *constant* time—matching the naive array-based solution—under a couple of assumptions that generally hold in practice (described in Section 12.3). A hash table uses space linear in the number of objects stored. This is radically less than the space required by the naive array-based solution, which is proportional to the number of all-imaginable objects that might ever need to be stored. The scorecard reads:

Operation	Typical running time
LOOKUP	$O(1)^*$
INSERT	$O(1)$
DELETE	$O(1)^*$

Table 12.1: Hash tables: supported operations and their typical running times. The asterisk (*) indicates that the running time bound holds if and only if the hash table is implemented properly (with a good hash function and an appropriate table size) and the data is non-pathological; see Section 12.3 for details.

Summarizing, hash tables don't support many operations, but what they do, they do really, really well. Whenever lookups constitute a significant amount of your program's work, a light bulb should go off in your head—the program calls out for a hash table!

When to Use a Hash Table

If your application requires fast lookups with a dynamically changing set of objects, the hash table is usually the data structure of choice.

12.1.1   Solution to Quiz 12.1

Correct answer: (c). The point of this quiz is to have fun thinking about some really big numbers, rather than to identify the correct answer per se. Let's assume that there are 26 choices for a character—ignoring punctuation, upper vs. lower case, etc. Then, there are 26^{25} 25-letter strings, which has order of magnitude roughly 10^{35}. (There are also the strings with 24 letters or less, but these are dwarfed by the length-25 strings.) The number of hairs on a person's head is typically around 10^5. The indexed Web has several billion pages, but the actual number of Web pages is probably around one trillion (10^{12}). The total amount of storage on Earth is hard to estimate but, at least in 2018, is surely no more than a yottabyte (10^{24} bytes, or roughly 10^{25} bits). Meanwhile, the number of atoms in the known universe is estimated to be around 10^{80}.

12.2   Applications

It's pretty amazing how many different applications boil down to repeated lookups and hence call out for a hash table. Back in the 1950s, researchers building the first compilers needed a *symbol table*, meaning a good data structure for keeping track of a program's variable and function names. Hash tables were invented for exactly this type of application. For a more modern example, imagine that a network router is tasked with blocking data packets from certain IP addresses, perhaps belonging to spammers. Every time a new data packet arrives, the router must look up whether the source IP address is in the blacklist. If so, it drops the packet; otherwise, it forwards the packet toward its destination. Again, these repeated lookups are right in the wheelhouse of hash tables.

12.2.1   Application: De-duplication

De-duplication is a canonical application of hash tables. Suppose you're processing a massive amount of data that's arriving one piece at a time, as a stream. For example:

- You're making a single pass over a huge file stored on disk, like all the transactions of a major retail company from the past year.

- You're crawling the Web and processing billions of Web pages.

- You're tracking data packets passing through a network router at a torrential rate.

- You're watching the visitors to your Web site.

In the de-duplication problem, your responsibility is to ignore duplicates and keep track only of the distinct keys seen so far. For example, you may be interested in the number of distinct IP addresses that have accessed your Web site, in addition to the total number of visits. Hash tables provide a simple solution to the de-duplication problem.

De-duplication with a Hash Table

When a new object x with key k arrives:

1. Use LOOKUP to check if the hash table already contains an object with key k.

2. If not, use INSERT to put x in the hash table.

After processing the data, the hash table contains exactly one object per key represented in the data stream.[1]

---

[1]With most hash table implementations, it's possible to iterate through the stored objects, in some arbitrary order, in linear time. This enables further processing of the objects after the duplicates have been removed.

12.2.2   Application: The 2-SUM Problem

Our next example is more academic, but it illustrates how repeated lookups can show up in surprising places. The example is about the 2-SUM problem.

Problem: 2-SUM

Input: An unsorted array A of n integers, and a target integer t.

Goal: Determine whether or not there are two numbers x, y in A satisfying $x + y = t$.[2]

The 2-SUM problem can be solved by brute-force search—by trying all possibilities for x and y and checking if any of them work. Because there are n choices for each of x and y, this is a quadratic-time ($\Theta(n^2)$) algorithm.

We can do better. The first key observation is that, for each choice of x, only one choice for y could possibly work (namely, $t - x$). So why not look specifically for this y?

2-SUM (Attempt #1)

Input: array A of n integers and a target integer t.
Output: "yes" if $A[i] + A[j] = t$ for some $i, j \in \{1, 2, 3, \ldots, n\}$, "no" otherwise.

---

for $i = 1$ to n **do**
$\quad y := t - A[i]$
$\quad$ **if** A contains y **then**   // linear search
$\quad\quad$ return "yes"
return "no"

Does this help? The for loop has n iterations and it takes linear time to search for an integer in an unsorted array, so this would seem to be

---

[2]There are two slightly different versions of the problem, depending on whether or not x and y are required to be distinct. We'll allow $x = y$; the other case is similar (as you should check).

another quadratic-time algorithm. But remember, sorting is a for-free primitive. Why not use it, so that all the searches can take advantage of a sorted array?

2-SUM (Sorted Array Solution)

Input: array A of n integers and a target integer t.
Output: "yes" if $A[i] + A[j] = t$ for some
$i, j \in \{1, 2, 3, \ldots, n\}$, "no" otherwise.

---

sort A // using a sorting subroutine
for $i = 1$ to n **do**
    $y := t - A[i]$
    if A contains y **then**   // binary search
        return "yes"
return "no"

Quiz 12.2

What's the running time of an educated implementation of the sorted array-based algorithm for the 2-SUM problem?

a) $\Theta(n)$

b) $\Theta(n \log n)$

c) $\Theta(n^{1.5})$

d) $\Theta(n^2)$

(See Section 12.2.4 for the solution and discussion.)

The sorted array-based solution to 2-SUM is a big improvement over brute-force search, and it showcases the elegant power of the algorithmic tools from *Part 1*. But we can do even better. The final insight is that this algorithm needed a sorted array only inasmuch as it needed to search it quickly. Because most of the work boils down to repeated lookups, a light bulb should go off in your head: A sorted array is overkill, and what this algorithm really calls out for is a hash table!

2-SUM (Hash Table Solution)

Input: array A of n integers and a target integer t.
Output: "yes" if $A[i] + A[j] = t$ for some
$i, j \in \{1, 2, 3, \ldots, n\}$, "no" otherwise.

$H :=$ empty hash table
for $i = 1$ to n **do**
    INSERT $A[i]$ into H
for $i = 1$ to n **do**
    $y := t - A[i]$
    if H contains y **then**   // using LOOKUP
        return "yes"
return "no"

Assuming a good hash table implementation and non-pathological data, the INSERT and LOOKUP operations typically run in constant time. In this case, the hash table-based solution to the 2-SUM problem runs in *linear* time. Because any correct algorithm must look at every number in A at least once, this is the best-possible running time (up to constant factors).

12.2.3 Application: Searching Huge State Spaces

Hash tables are all about speeding up search. One application domain in which search is ubiquitous is game-playing, and more generally in planning problems. Think, for example, of a chess-playing program exploring the ramifications of different moves. Sequences of moves can be viewed as paths in a huge directed graph, where vertices correspond to states of the game (positions of all the pieces and whose turn it is), and edges correspond to moves (from one state to another). The size of this graph is astronomical (more than 10^{100} vertices), so there's no hope of writing it down explicitly and applying any of our graph search algorithms from Chapter 8. A more tractable alternative is to run a graph search algorithm like breadth-first search, starting from the current state, and explore the short-term consequences of different moves until reaching a time limit. To learn as much as possible, it's important to avoid exploring a vertex more than once, and so the search algorithm must keep track of which vertices it has already

visited. As in our de-duplication application, this task is ready-made
for a hash table. When the search algorithm reaches a vertex, it looks
it up in a hash table. If the vertex is already there, the algorithm
skips it and backtracks; otherwise, it inserts the vertex into the hash
table and proceeds with its exploration.[3,4]

12.2.4   Solution to Quiz 12.2

Correct answer: (b). The first step can be implemented in
$O(n \log n)$ time using MergeSort (described in *Part 1*) or HeapSort
(Section 10.3.1).[5] Each of the n for loop iterations can be implemented
in $O(\log n)$ time via binary search. Adding everything up gives the
final running time bound of $O(n \log n)$.

*12.3   Implementation: High-Level Ideas

This section covers the most important high-level ideas in a hash table
implementation: hash functions (which map keys to positions in an
array), collisions (different keys that map to the same position), and
the most common collision-resolution strategies. Section 12.4 offers
more detailed advice about implementing a hash table.

12.3.1   Two Straightforward Solutions

A hash table stores a set S of keys (and associated data), drawn from
a universe U of all possible keys. For example, U might be all 2^{32}
possible IPv4 addresses, all possible strings of length at most 25, all
possible chess board states, and so on. The set S could be the IP
addresses that actually visited a Web page in the last 24 hours, the
actual names of your friends, or the chess board states that your

---

[3]In game-playing applications, the most popular graph search algorithm is
called A^* *("A star") search.* The A^* search algorithm is a goal-oriented general-
ization of Dijkstra's algorithm (Chapter 9), which adds to the Dijkstra score (9.1)
of an edge (v, w) a heuristic estimate of the cost required to travel from w to a
"goal vertex." For example, if you're computing driving directions from a given
origin to a given destination t, the heuristic estimate could be the straight-line
distance from w to t.

[4]Take a moment to think about modern technology and speculate where else
hash tables are used. It shouldn't take long to come up with some good guesses!

[5]No faster implementation is possible, at least with a comparison-based sorting
algorithm (see footnote 10 in Chapter 10).

program explored in the last five seconds. In most applications of hash tables, the size of U is astronomical but the size of the subset S is manageable.

One conceptually straightforward way to implement the LOOKUP, INSERT, and DELETE operations is to keep track of objects in a big array, with one entry for every possible key in U. If U is a small set like all three-character strings (to keep track of airports by their three-letter codes, say), this array-based solution is a good one, with all operations running in constant time. In the many applications in which U is extremely large, this solution is absurd and unimplementable; we can realistically consider only data structures requiring space proportional to $|S|$ (rather than to $|U|$).

A second straightforward solution is to store objects in a linked list. The good news is that the space this solution uses is proportional to $|S|$. The bad news is that the running times of LOOKUP and DELETE also scale linearly with $|S|$—far worse than the constant-time operations that the array-based solution supports. The point of a hash table is to achieve the best of both worlds—space proportional to $|S|$ and constant-time operations (Table 12.2).

Data Structure	Space	Typical Running Time of LOOKUP
Array	$\Theta(|U|)$	$\Theta(1)$
Linked List	$\Theta(|S|)$	$\Theta(|S|)$
Hash Table	$\Theta(|S|)$	$\Theta(1)^*$

Table 12.2: Hash tables combine the best features of arrays and linked lists, with space linear in the number of objects stored and constant-time operations. The asterisk (*) indicates that the running time bound holds if and only if the hash table is implemented properly and the data is non-pathological.

12.3.2 Hash Functions

To achieve the best of both worlds, a hash table mimics the straightforward array-based solution, but with the array length n proportional to $|S|$ rather than $|U|$.[6] For now, you can think of n as roughly $2|S|$.

---

[6]But wait; isn't the set S changing over time? Yes it is, but it's not hard to periodically resize the array so that its length remains proportional to the current size of S; see also Section 12.4.2.

A *hash function* performs the translation from what we really care about—our friends' names, chess board states, etc.—to positions in the hash table. Formally, a hash function is a function from the set U of all possible keys to the set of array positions (Figure 12.2). Positions are usually numbered from 0 in a hash table, so the set of array positions is $\{0, 1, 2, \ldots, n-1\}$.

Hash Functions

A hash function $h : U \to \{0, 1, 2, \ldots, n-1\}$ assigns every key from the universe U to a position in an array of length n.

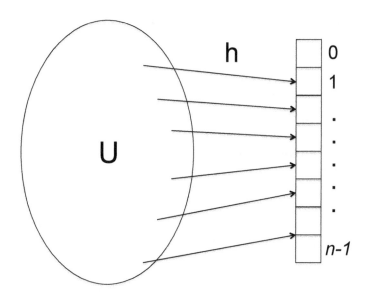

Figure 12.2: A hash function maps every possible key in the universe U to a position in $\{0, 1, 2, \ldots, n-1\}$. When $|U| > n$, two different keys must be mapped to the same position.

A hash function tells you where to start searching for an object. If you choose a hash function h with $h(\text{"Alice"}) = 17$—in which case, we say that the string "Alice" *hashes* to 17—then position 17 of the array is the place to start looking for Alice's phone number. Similarly, position 17 is the first place to try inserting Alice's phone number into the hash table.

12.3.3   Collisions Are Inevitable

You may have noticed a serious issue: What if two different keys (like "Alice" and "Bob") hash to the same position (like 23)? If you're looking for Alice's phone number but find Bob's in position 23 of the array, how do you know whether or not Alice's number is also in the hash table? If you're trying to insert Alice's phone number into position 23 but the position is already occupied, where do you put it?

When a hash function h maps two different keys k_1 and k_2 to the same position (that is, when $h(k_1) = h(k_2)$), it's called a *collision*.

Collisions

Two keys k_1 and k_2 from U *collide* under the hash function h if $h(k_1) = h(k_2)$.

Collisions cause confusion about where an object resides in the hash table, and we'd like to minimize them as much as possible. Why not design a super-smart hash function with no collisions whatsoever? Because *collisions are inevitable*. The reason is the *Pigeonhole Principle*, the intuitively obvious fact that, for every positive integer n, no matter how you stuff $n + 1$ pigeons into n holes, there will be a hole with at least two pigeons. Thus whenever the number n of array positions (the holes) is less than the size of the universe U (the pigeons), every hash function (assignment of pigeons to holes)—no matter how clever—suffers from at least one collision (Figure 12.2). In most applications of hash tables, including those in Section 12.2, $|U|$ is much, much bigger than n.

Collisions are even more inevitable than the Pigeonhole Principle argument suggests. The reason is the *birthday paradox*, the subject of the next quiz.

Quiz 12.3

Consider n people with random birthdays, with each of the 366 days of the year equally likely. (Assume all n people were born in a leap year.) How large does n need to be before there is at least a 50% chance that two people have the same birthday?

---

a) 23

b) 57

c) 184

d) 367

(See Section 12.3.7 for the solution and discussion.)

What does the birthday paradox have to do with hashing? Imagine a hash function that assigns each key independently and uniformly at random to a position in $\{0, 1, 2, \ldots, n - 1\}$. This is not a practically viable hash function (see Quiz 12.5), but such random functions are the gold standard to which we compare practical hash functions (see Section 12.3.6). The birthday paradox implies that, even for the gold standard, we're likely to start seeing collisions in a hash table of size n once a small constant times $\sqrt{n}$ objects have been inserted. For example, when $n = 10,000$, the insertion of 200 objects is likely to cause at least one collision—even though at least 98% of the array positions are completely unused!

12.3.4   Collision Resolution: Chaining

With collisions an inevitable fact of life, a hash table needs some method for resolving them. This section and the next describe the two dominant approaches, *separate chaining* (or simply *chaining*) and *open addressing*. Both approaches lead to implementations in which insertions and lookups typically run in constant time, assuming the hash table size and hash function are chosen appropriately and the data is non-pathological (cf., Table 12.1).

Buckets and Lists

Chaining is easy to implement and think about. The key idea is to default to the linked-list-based solution (Section 12.3.1) to handle multiple objects mapped to the same array position (Figure 12.3). With chaining, the positions of the array are often called *buckets*, as each can contain multiple objects. The LOOKUP, INSERT, and DELETE operations then reduce to one hash function evaluation (to determine the correct bucket) and the corresponding linked list operation.

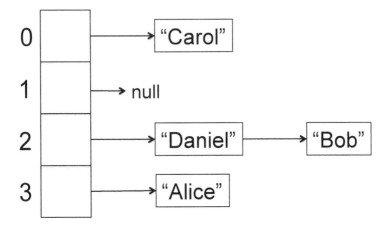

Figure 12.3: A hash table with collisions resolved by chaining, with four buckets and four objects. The strings "Bob" and "Daniel" collide in the third bucket (bucket 2). Only the keys are shown, and not the associated data (like phone numbers).

Chaining

1. Keep a linked list in each bucket of the hash table.

2. To LOOKUP/INSERT/DELETE an object with key k, perform LOOKUP/INSERT DELETE on the linked list in the bucket $A[h(k)]$, where h denotes the hash function and A the hash table's array.

Performance of Chaining

Provided h can be evaluated in constant time, the INSERT operation also takes constant time—the new object can be inserted immediately at the front of the list. LOOKUP and DELETE must search through the list stored in $A[h(k)]$, which takes time proportional to the list's length. To achieve constant-time lookups in a hash table with chaining, the buckets' lists must stay short—ideally, with length at most a small constant.

List lengths (and lookup times) degrade if the hash table becomes heavily populated. For example, if $100n$ objects are stored in a hash table with array length n, a typical bucket has 100 objects to sift through. Lookup times can also degrade with a poorly chosen hash function that causes lots of collisions. For example, in the extreme case in which all the objects collide and wind up in the same bucket, lookups can take time linear in the data set size. Section 12.4 elaborates on how to manage the size of a hash table and choose an appropriate hash function to achieve the running time bounds stated in Table 12.1.

12.3.5   Collision Resolution: Open Addressing

The second popular method for resolving collisions is *open addressing*. Open addressing is much easier to implement and understand when the hash table must support only INSERT and LOOKUP (and not DELETE); we'll focus on this case.[7]

With open addressing, each position of the array stores 0 or 1 objects, rather than a list. (For this to make sense, the size $|S|$ of the data set cannot exceed the size n of the hash table.) Collisions create an immediate quandary for the INSERT operation: Where do we put an object with key k if a different object is already stored in the position $A[h(k)]$?

Probe Sequences

The idea is to associate each key k with a *probe sequence* of positions, not just a single position. The first number of the sequence indicates the position to consider first; the second the next position to consider when the first is already occupied; and so on. The object is stored in the first unoccupied position of its key's probe sequence (see Figure 12.4).

Open Addressing

1. INSERT: Given an object with key k, iterate through the probe sequence associated with k, storing the object in the first empty position found.

---

[7]Plenty of hash table applications don't require the DELETE operation, including the three applications in Section 12.2.

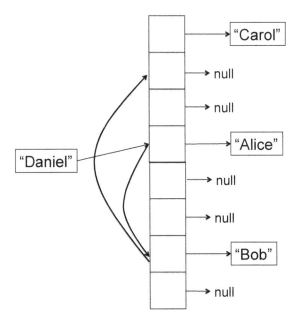

Figure 12.4: An insertion into a hash table with collisions resolved by open addressing. The first entry of the probe sequence for "Daniel" collides with "Alice," and the second with "Bob," but the third entry is an unoccupied position.

2. LOOKUP: Given a key k, iterate through the probe sequence associated with k until encountering the desired object (in which case, return it) or an empty position (in which case, report "none").[8]

Linear Probing

There are several ways to use one or more hash functions to define a probe sequence. The simplest is *linear probing*. This method uses one hash function h, and defines the probe sequence for a key k as $h(k)$, followed by $h(k)+1$, followed by $h(k)+2$, and so on (wrapping around to the beginning upon reaching the last position). That is, the hash

---

[8]If you encounter an empty position i, you can be confident that no object with key k is in the hash table. Such an object would have been stored either at position i or at an earlier position in k's probe sequence.

function indicates the starting position for an insertion or lookup, and the operation scans to the right until it finds the desired object or an empty position.

Double Hashing

A more sophisticated method is *double hashing*, which uses two hash functions.[9] The first tells you the first position of the probe sequence, and the second indicates the offset for subsequent positions. For example, if $h_1(k) = 17$ and $h_2(k) = 23$, the first place to look for an object with key k is position 17; failing that, position 40; failing that, position 63; failing that, position 86; and so on. For a different key k', the probe sequence could look quite different. For example, if $h_1(k') = 42$ and $h_2(k') = 27$, the probe sequence would be 42, followed by 69, followed by 96, followed by 123, and so on.

Performance of Open Addressing

With chaining, the running time of a lookup is governed by the lengths of buckets' lists; with open addressing, it's the typical number of probes required to find either an empty slot or the sought-after object. It's harder to understand hash table performance with open addressing than with chaining, but it should be intuitively clear that performance suffers as the hash table gets increasingly full—if very few slots are empty, it will usually take a probe sequence a long time to find one—or when a poor choice of hash function causes lots of collisions (see also Quiz 12.4). With an appropriate hash table size and hash function, open addressing achieves the running time bounds stated in Table 12.1 for the INSERT and LOOKUP operations; see Section 12.4 for additional details.

12.3.6   What Makes for a Good Hash Function?

No matter which collision-resolution strategy we employ, hash table performance degrades with the number of collisions. How can we choose a hash function so that there aren't too many collisions?

---

[9]There are several quick-and-dirty ways to define two hash functions from a single hash function h. For example, if keys are nonnegative integers represented in binary, define h_1 and h_2 from h by tacking on a new digit (either '0' or '1') to the end of the given key k: $h_1(k) = h(2k)$ and $h_2(k) = h(2k + 1)$.

Bad Hash Functions

There are a zillion different ways to define a hash function, and the choice matters. For example, what happens to hash table performance with a dumbest-possible choice of a hash function?

Quiz 12.4

Consider a hash table with length $n \geq 1$, and let h be the hash function with $h(k) = 0$ for every key $k \in U$. Suppose a data set S is inserted into the hash table, with $|S| \leq n$. What is the typical running time of subsequent LOOKUP operations?

a) $\Theta(1)$ with chaining, $\Theta(1)$ with open addressing.

b) $\Theta(1)$ with chaining, $\Theta(|S|)$ with open addressing.

c) $\Theta(|S|)$ with chaining, $\Theta(1)$ with open addressing.

d) $\Theta(|S|)$ with chaining, $\Theta(|S|)$ with open addressing.

(See Section 12.3.7 for the solution and discussion.)

Pathological Data Sets and Hash Function Kryptonite

None of us would ever implement the dumb hash function in Quiz 12.4. Instead, we'd work hard to design a smart hash function guaranteed to cause few collisions, or better yet to look up such a function in a book like this one. Unfortunately, I can't tell you such a function. My excuse? *Every hash function, no matter how smart, has its own kryptonite,* in the form of a huge data set for which all objects collide and with hash table performance deteriorating as in Quiz 12.4.

Pathological Data Sets

For *every* hash function $h : U \to \{0, 1, 2, \ldots, n-1\}$, there exists a set S of keys of size $|U|/n$ such that $h(k_1) = h(k_2)$ for every $k_1, k_2 \in S$.[10]

This may sound crazy, but it's just a generalization of our Pigeonhole Principle argument from Section 12.3.3. Fix an arbitrarily smart hash function h. If h perfectly partitions the keys in U among the n positions, then each position would have exactly $|U|/n$ keys assigned to it; otherwise, even more than $|U|/n$ keys are assigned to the same position. (For example, if $|U| = 200$ and $n = 25$, then h must assign at least eight different keys to the same position.) In any case, there is a position $i \in \{0, 1, 2, \ldots, n - 1\}$ to which h assigns at least $|U|/n$ distinct keys. If the keys in a data set S happen to be all those assigned to this position i, then all the objects in the data set collide.

The data set S above is "pathological" in that it was constructed with the sole purpose of foiling the chosen hash function. Why should we care about such an artificial data set? The main reason is that it explains the asterisks in our running time bounds for hash table operations in Tables 12.1 and 12.2. Unlike most of the algorithms and data structures we've seen so far, there is no hope for a running time guarantee that holds with absolutely no assumptions about the input. The best we can hope for is a guarantee that applies to all "non-pathological" data sets, meaning data sets defined independently of the chosen hash function.[11]

The good news is that, with a well-crafted hash function, there's usually no need to worry about pathological data sets in practice. Security applications constitute an important exception to this rule, however.[12]

Random Hash Functions

Pathological data sets show that no one hash function is guaranteed to have a small number of collisions for every data set. The best

---

[10]In most applications of hash tables, $|U|$ is way bigger than n, in which case a data set of size $|U|/n$ is huge!

[11]It is also possible to consider randomized solutions, in the spirit of the randomized QuickSort algorithm in Chapter 5 of *Part 1*. This approach, called *universal hashing*, guarantees that for *every* data set, a random choice of a hash function from a small class of functions typically causes few collisions. For details and examples, see the bonus videos at www.algorithmsilluminated.org.

[12]An interesting case study is described in the paper "Denial of Service via Algorithmic Complexity Attacks," by Scott A. Crosby and Dan S. Wallach (*Proceedings of the 12th USENIX Security Symposium*, 2003). Crosby and Wallach showed how to bring a hash table-based network intrusion system to its knees through the clever construction of a pathological data set.

we can hope for is a hash function that has few collisions for all "non-pathological" data sets.[13]

An extreme approach to decorrelating the choice of hash function and the data set is to choose a random function, meaning a function h where, for each key $k \in U$, the value of $h(k)$ is chosen independently and uniformly at random from the array positions $\{0, 1, 2, \ldots, n - 1\}$. The function h is chosen once and for all when the hash table is initially created. Intuitively, we'd expect such a random function to typically spread out the objects of a data set S roughly evenly across the n positions, provided S is defined independently of h. As long as n is roughly equal to $|S|$, this would result in a manageable number of collisions.

Quiz 12.5

Why is it impractical to use a completely random choice of a hash function? (Choose all that apply.)

a) Actually, it is practical.

b) It is not deterministic.

c) It would take too much space to store.

d) It would take too much time to evaluate.

(See Section 12.3.7 for the solution and discussion.)

Good Hash Functions

A "good" hash function is one that enjoys the benefits of a random function without suffering from either of its drawbacks.

Hash Function Desiderata

1. Cheap to evaluate, ideally in $O(1)$ time.

2. Easy to store, ideally with $O(1)$ memory.

---

[13]The dumb hash function in Quiz 12.4 leads to terrible performance for *every* data set, pathological or otherwise.

> 3. Mimics a random function by spreading non-pathological data sets roughly evenly across the positions of the hash table.

What Does a Good Hash Function Look Like?

While a detailed description of state-of-the-art hash functions is outside the scope of this book, you might be hungry for something more concrete than the desiderata above.

For example, consider keys that are integers between 0 and some large number M.[14] A natural first stab at a hash function is to take a key's value modulo the number n of buckets:

$$h(k) = k \bmod n,$$

where $k \bmod n$ is the result of repeatedly subtracting n from k until the result is an integer between 0 and $n - 1$.

The good news is that this function is cheap to evaluate and requires no storage (beyond remembering n).[15] The bad news is that many real-world sets of keys are not uniformly distributed in their least significant bits. For example, if $n = 1000$ and all the keys have the same last three digits (base 10)—perhaps salaries at a company that are all multiples of 1000, or prices of cars that all end in "999"— then all the keys are hashed to the same position. Using only the most significant bits can cause similar problems—think, for example, about the country and area codes of phone numbers.

The next idea is to scramble a key before applying the modulus operation:

$$h(k) = (ak + b) \bmod n,$$

where a and b are integers in $\{1, 2, \ldots, n - 1\}$. This function is again cheap to compute and easy to store (just remember a, b, and n). For well-chosen a, b, and n, this function is probably good enough to use in a quick-and-dirty prototype. For mission-critical code, however, it's often essential to use more sophisticated hash functions, which are discussed further in Section 12.4.3.

---

[14]To apply this idea to non-numerical data like strings, it's necessary to first convert the data to integers. For example, in Java, the `hashCode` method implements such a conversion.

[15]There are much faster ways to compute $k \bmod n$ than repeated subtraction!

To conclude, the two most important things to know about hash function design are:

Take-Aways

1. Experts have invented hash functions that are cheap to evaluate and easy to store, and that behave like random functions for all practical purposes.

2. Designing such a hash function is extremely tricky; you should leave it to experts if at all possible.

12.3.7 Solutions to Quizzes 12.3—12.5

Solution to Quiz 12.3

Correct answer: (a). Believe it or not, all you need is 23 people in a room before it's as likely to have two with the same birthday as not.[16] You can do (or look up) the appropriate probability calculation, or convince yourself of this with some simple simulations.

With 367 people, there would be a 100% chance of two people with the same birthday (by the Pigeonhole Principle). But already with 57 people, the probability is roughly 99%. And with 184? 99.99...%, with a large number of nines.

Most people find the answer counterintuitive; this is why the example is known as the "birthday paradox."[17] More generally, on a planet with k days each year, the chance of duplicate birthdays hits 50% with $\Theta(\sqrt{k})$ people.[18]

---

[16] A good party trick at not-so-nerdy cocktail parties with at least, say, 35 people.

[17] "Paradox" is a misnomer here; there's no logical inconsistency, just another illustration of how most people's brains are not wired to have good intuition about probability.

[18] The reason is that n people represent not just n opportunities for duplicate birthdays, but $\binom{n}{2} \approx \frac{n^2}{2}$ different opportunities (one for each pair of people). Two people have the same birthday with probability $\frac{1}{k}$, and you expect to start seeing collisions once the number of collision opportunities is roughly k (when $n = \Theta(\sqrt{k})$).

Solution to Quiz 12.4

Correct answer: (d). If collisions are resolved with chaining, the hash function h hashes every object in S to the same bucket: bucket 0. The hash table devolves into the simple linked-list solution, with $\Theta(|S|)$ time required for LOOKUP.

For the case of open addressing, assume that the hash table uses linear probing. (The story is the same for more complicated strategies like double hashing.) The lucky first object of $|S|$ will be assigned to position 0 of the array, the next object to position 1, and so on. The LOOKUP operation devolves to a linear search through the first $|S|$ positions of an unsorted array, which requires $\Theta(|S|)$ time.

Solution to Quiz 12.5

Correct answers: (c),(d). A random function from U to $\{0, 1, 2, \ldots, n-1\}$ is effectively a lookup table of length $|U|$ with $\log_2 n$ bits per entry. When the universe is large (as in most applications), writing down or evaluating such a function is out of the question.

We could try defining the hash function on a need-to-know basis, assigning a random value to $h(k)$ the first time the key k is encountered. But then evaluating $h(k)$ requires first checking whether it has already been defined. This boils down to a lookup for k, which is the problem we're supposed to be solving!

*12.4   Further Implementation Details

This section is for readers who want to implement a custom hash table from scratch. There's no silver bullet in hash table design, so I can only offer high-level guidance. The most important lessons are: (i) manage your hash table's load; (ii) use a well-tested modern hash function; and (iii) test several competing implementations to determine the best one for your particular application.

12.4.1   Load vs. Performance

The performance of a hash table degrades as its population increases: with chaining, buckets' lists grow longer; with open addressing, it gets harder to locate an empty slot.

The Load of a Hash Table

We measure the population of a hash table via its *load*:

$$\text{load of a hash table} = \frac{\text{number of objects stored}}{\text{array length } n}. \tag{12.1}$$

For example, in a hash table with chaining, the load is the average population in one of the table's buckets.

Quiz 12.6

Which hash table strategy is feasible for loads larger than 1?

a) Both chaining and open addressing.

b) Neither chaining nor open addressing.

c) Only chaining.

d) Only open addressing.

(See Section 12.4.5 for the solution and discussion.)

Idealized Performance with Chaining

In a hash table with chaining, the running time of a LOOKUP or DELETE operation scales with the lengths of buckets' lists. In the best-case scenario, the hash function spreads the objects perfectly evenly across the buckets. With a load of α, this idealized scenario results in at most $\lceil \alpha \rceil$ objects per bucket.[19] The LOOKUP and DELETE operations then take only $O(\lceil \alpha \rceil)$ time, and so are constant-time operations provided $\alpha = O(1)$.[20] Since good hash functions spread most data sets roughly evenly across buckets, this best-case performance is approximately matched by practical chaining-based hash table im-

---

[19]The notation $\lceil x \rceil$ denotes the "ceiling" function, which rounds its argument up to the nearest integer.

[20]We bother to write $O(\lceil \alpha \rceil)$ instead of $O(\alpha)$ only to handle the case where α is close to 0. The running time of every operation is always $\Omega(1)$, no matter how small α is—if nothing else, there is one hash function evaluation to be accounted for. Alternatively, we could write $O(1 + \alpha)$ in place of $O(\lceil \alpha \rceil)$.

plementations (with a good hash function and with non-pathological data).[21]

Idealized Performance with Open Addressing

In a hash table with open addressing, the running time of a LOOKUP or INSERT operation scales with the number of probes required to locate an empty slot (or the sought-after object). When the hash table's load is α, an α fraction of its slots are full and the remaining $1 - \alpha$ fraction are empty. In the best-case scenario, each probe is uncorrelated with the hash table's contents and has a $1 - \alpha$ chance of locating an empty slot. In this idealized scenario, the expected number of probes required is $\frac{1}{1-\alpha}$.[22] If α is bounded away from 1—like 70%, for example—the idealized running time of all operations is $O(1)$. This best-case performance is approximately matched by practical hash tables implemented with double hashing or other sophisticated probe sequences. With linear probing, objects tend to clump together in consecutive slots, resulting in slower operation times: roughly $\frac{1}{(1-\alpha)^2}$, even in the idealized case.[23] This is still $O(1)$ time provided α is significantly less than 100%.

---

[21] Here's a more mathematical argument for readers who remember basic probability. A good hash function mimics a random function, so let's go ahead and assume that the hash function h independently assigns each key to one of the n buckets uniformly at random. (See Section 12.6.1 for further discussion of this heuristic assumption.) Suppose that all objects' keys are distinct, and that the key k is mapped to position i by h. Under our assumption, for every other key k' represented in the hash table, the probability that h also maps k' to the position i is $1/n$. In total over the $|S|$ keys in the data set S, the expected number of keys that share k's bucket is $|S|/n$, a quantity known also as the load α. (Technically, this follows from linearity of expectation and the "decomposition blueprint" described in Section 5.5 of *Part 1*.) The expected running time of a LOOKUP for an object with key k is therefore $O(\lceil \alpha \rceil)$.

[22] This is like a coin-flipping experiment: if a coin has probability p of coming up "heads," what is the average number of flips required to see your first "heads?" (For us, $p = 1 - \alpha$.) As discussed in Section 6.2 of *Part 1*—or search Wikipedia for "geometric random variable"—the answer is $\frac{1}{p}$.

[23] This highly non-obvious result was first derived by Donald E. Knuth, the father of the analysis of algorithms. It made quite an impression on him: "I first formulated the following derivation in 1962... Ever since that day, the analysis of algorithms has in fact been one of the major themes in my life." (Donald E. Knuth, *The Art of Computer Programming, Volume 3 (2nd edition)*, Addison-Wesley, 1998, page 536.)

Collision-Resolution Strategy	Idealized Running Time of LOOKUP
Chaining	$O\left(\lceil \alpha \rceil\right)$
Double hashing	$O\left(\frac{1}{1-\alpha}\right)$
Linear probing	$O\left(\frac{1}{(1-\alpha)^2}\right)$

Table 12.3: Idealized performance of a hash table as a function of its load α and its collision-resolution strategy.[24]

12.4.2 Managing the Load of Your Hash Table

Insertions and deletions change the numerator in (12.1), and a hash table implementation should update the denominator to keep pace. A good rule of thumb is to periodically resize the hash table's array so that the table's load stays below 70% (or perhaps even less, depending on the application and your collision-resolution strategy). Then, with a well-chosen hash function and non-pathological data, all of the most common collision-resolution strategies typically lead to constant-time hash table operations.

The simplest way to implement array resizing is to keep track of the table's load and, whenever it reaches 70%, to double the number n of buckets. All the objects are then rehashed into the new, larger hash table (which now has load 35%). Optionally, if a sequence of deletions brings the load down far enough, the array can be downsized accordingly to save space (with all remaining objects rehashed into the smaller table). Such resizes can be time-consuming, but in most applications they are infrequent.

12.4.3 Choosing Your Hash Function

Designing good hash functions is a difficult and dark art. It's easy to propose reasonable-looking hash functions that end up being subtly flawed, leading to poor hash table performance. For this reason, I advise against designing your own hash functions from scratch. Fortunately, a number of clever programmers have devised an array

---

[24]For more details on how the performance of different collision-resolution strategies varies with the hash table load, see the bonus videos at www.algorithmsilluminated.org.

of well-tested and publicly available hash functions that you can use in your own work.

Which hash function should you use? Ask ten programmers this question, and you'll get at least eleven different answers. Because different hash functions fare better on different data distributions, you should compare the performance of several state-of-the-art hash functions in your particular application and runtime environment. As of this writing (in 2018), hash functions that are good starting points for further exploration include `FarmHash`, `MurmurHash3`, `SpookyHash` and `MD5`. These are all *non-cryptographic* hash functions, and are not designed to protect against adversarial attacks like that of Crosby and Wallach (see footnote 12).[25] *Cryptographic* hash functions are more complicated and slower to evaluate than their non-cryptographic counterparts, but they do protect against such attacks.[26] A good starting point here is the hash function `SHA-1` and its newer relatives like `SHA-256`.

12.4.4   Choosing Your Collision-Resolution Strategy

For collision resolution, is it better to use chaining or open addressing? With open addressing, is it better to use linear probing, double hashing, or something else? As usual, when I present you with multiple solutions to a problem, the answer is "it depends." For example, chaining takes more space than open addressing (to store the pointers in the linked lists), so the latter might be preferable when space is a first-order concern. Deletions are more complicated with open addressing than with chaining, so chaining might be preferable in applications with lots of deletions.

Comparing linear probing with more complicated open addressing implementations like double hashing is also tricky. Linear probing results in bigger clumps of consecutive objects in the hash table and therefore more probes than more sophisticated approaches; however, this cost can be offset by its friendly interactions with the runtime

---

[25]`MD5` was originally designed to be a cryptographic hash function, but it is no longer considered secure.

[26]All hash functions, even cryptographic ones, have pathological data sets (Section 12.3.6). Cryptographic hash functions have the special property that it's computationally infeasible to reverse engineer a pathological data set, in the same sense that it's computationally infeasible to factor large integers and break the RSA public-key cryptosystem.

environment's memory hierarchy. As with the choice of a hash function, for mission-critical code, there's no substitute for coding up multiple competing implementations and seeing which works best for your application.

12.4.5 Solution to Quiz 12.6

Correct answer: (c). Because hash tables with open addressing store at most one object per array position, they can never have a load larger than 1. Once the load is 1, it's not possible to insert any more objects.

An arbitrary number of objects can be inserted into a hash table with chaining, although performance degrades as more are inserted. For example, if the load is 100, the average length of a bucket's list is also 100.

12.5 Bloom Filters: The Basics

Bloom filters are close cousins of hash tables.[27] They are ridiculously space-efficient but, in exchange, they occasionally make errors. This section covers what bloom filters are good for and how they are implemented, while Section 12.6 maps out the trade-off curve between a filter's space usage and its frequency of errors.

12.5.1 Supported Operations

The raison d'être of a bloom filter is essentially the same as that of a hash table: super-fast insertions and lookups, so that you can quickly remember what you've seen and what you haven't. Why should we bother with another data structure with the same set of operations? Because bloom filters are preferable to hash tables in applications in which space is at a premium and the occasional error is not a dealbreaker.

Like hash tables with open addressing, bloom filters are much easier to implement and understand when they support only INSERT and LOOKUP (and no DELETE). We'll focus on this case.

---

[27]Named after their inventor; see the paper "Space/Time Trade-offs in Hash Coding with Allowable Errors," by Burton H. Bloom (*Communications of the ACM*, 1970).

Bloom Filters: Supported Operations

LOOKUP: for a key k, return "yes" if k has been previously inserted into the bloom filter and "no" otherwise.

INSERT: add a new key k to the bloom filter.

Bloom filters are very space-efficient; in a typical use case, they might require only 8 bits per insertion. This is pretty incredible, as 8 bits are nowhere near enough to remember even a 32-bit key or a pointer to an object! This is the reason why the LOOKUP operation in a bloom filter returns only a "yes"/"no" answer, whereas in a hash table the operation returns a pointer to the sought-after object (if found). This is also why the INSERT operation now takes only a key, rather than (a pointer to) an object.

Bloom filters can make mistakes, in contrast to all the other data structures we've studied. There are two different kinds of mistakes: false negatives, in which LOOKUP returns "false" even though the queried key was inserted previously; and false positives, in which LOOKUP returns "true" even though the queried key was never inserted in the past. We'll see in Section 12.5.3 that basic bloom filters never suffer from false negatives, but they can have "phantom elements" in the form of false positives. Section 12.6 shows that the frequency of false positives can be controlled by tuning the space usage appropriately. A typical bloom filter implementation might have an error rate of around 1% or 0.1%.

The running times of both the INSERT and LOOKUP operations are as fast as those in a hash table. Even better, these operations are *guaranteed* to run in constant time, independent of the bloom filter implementation and the data set.[28] The implementation and data set do affect the filter's error rate, however.

Summarizing the advantages and disadvantages of bloom filters over hash tables:

Bloom Filters Vs. Hash Tables

1. **Pro:** More space efficient.

---

[28]Provided hash function evaluations take constant time and that a constant number of bits is used per inserted key.

2. **Pro:** Guaranteed constant-time operations for every data set.

3. **Con:** Can't store pointers to objects.

4. **Con:** Deletions are complicated, relative to a hash table with chaining.

5. **Con:** Non-zero false positive probability.

The scorecard for the basic bloom filter reads:

Operation	Running time
LOOKUP	$O(1)^\dagger$
INSERT	$O(1)$

Table 12.4: Basic bloom filters: supported operations and their running times. The dagger (†) indicates that the LOOKUP operation suffers from a controllable but non-zero probability of false positives.

Bloom filters should be used in place of hash tables in applications in which their advantages matter and their disadvantages are not dealbreakers.

When to Use a Bloom Filter

If your application requires fast lookups with a dynamically changing set of objects, space is at a premium, and a small number of false positives can be tolerated, the bloom filter is usually the data structure of choice.

12.5.2 Applications

Next are three applications with repeated lookups where it can be important to save space and where false positives are not a dealbreaker.

Spell checkers. Back in the 1970s, bloom filters were used to implement spell checkers. In a preprocessing step, every word in a dictionary was inserted into a bloom filter. Spell-checking a document boiled down to one LOOKUP operation per word in the document, flagging any words for which the operation returned "no."

In this application, a false positive corresponds to an illegal word that the spell checker inadvertently accepts. Such errors are not ideal. Space was at a premium in the early 1970s, however, so at that time it was a win to use bloom filters.

Forbidden passwords. An old application that remains relevant today is keeping track of forbidden passwords—passwords that are too common or too easy to guess. Initially, all forbidden passwords are inserted into a bloom filter; additional forbidden passwords can be inserted later, as needed. When a user tries to set or reset their password, the system looks up the proposed password in the bloom filter. If the LOOKUP returns "yes," the user is asked to try again with a different password. Here, a false positive translates to a strong password that the system rejects. Provided the error rate is not too large, say at most 1% or 0.1%, this is not a big deal. Once in a while, some user will need one extra attempt to find a password acceptable to the system.

Internet routers. Many of today's killer applications of bloom filters take place in the core of the Internet, where data packets pass through routers at a torrential rate. There are many reasons why a router might want to quickly recall what it has seen in the past. For example, the router might want to look up the source IP address of a packet in a list of blocked IP addresses, keep track of the contents of a cache to avoid spurious cache lookups, or maintain statistics helpful for identifying a denial-of-service attack. The rate of packet arrivals demands super-fast lookups, and limited router memory puts space at a premium. These applications are right in the wheelhouse of a bloom filter.

12.5.3   Implementation

Looking under the hood of a bloom filter reveals an elegant implementation. The data structure maintains an n-bit string, or equivalently a length-n array A in which each entry is either 0 or 1. (All entries are initialized to 0.) The structure also uses m hash functions $h_1, h_2, \ldots, h_m$, each mapping the universe U of all possible keys to the set $\{0, 1, 2, \ldots, n-1\}$ of array positions. The parameter m is proportional to the number of bits that the bloom filter uses per insertion, and is typically a small constant (like 5).[29]

Every time a key is inserted into a bloom filter, each of the m hash functions plants a flag by setting the corresponding bit of the array A to 1.

Bloom Filter: INSERT (given key k)

for $i = 1$ to m **do**
$\quad A[h_i(k)] := 1$

For example, if $m = 3$ and $h_1(k) = 23$, $h_2(k) = 17$, and $h_3(k) = 5$, inserting k causes the 5th, 17th, and 23rd bits of the array to be set to 1 (Figure 12.5).

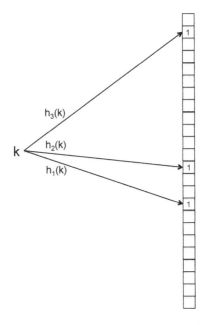

Figure 12.5: Inserting a new key k into a bloom filter sets the bits in positions $h_1(k), \ldots, h_m(k)$ to 1.

---

[29]Sections 12.3.6 and 12.4.3 provide guidance for choosing one hash function. Footnote 9 describes a quick-and-dirty way of deriving two hash functions from one; the same idea can be used to derive m hash functions from one. An alternative approach, inspired by double hashing, is to use two hash functions h and h' to define $h_1, h_2, \ldots, h_m$ via the formula $h_i(k) = (h(k) + (i - 1) \cdot h'(k)) \bmod n$.

In the LOOKUP operation, a bloom filter looks for the footprint that would have been left by k's insertion.

Bloom Filter: LOOKUP (given key k)

for $i = 1$ to m **do**
    if $A[h_i(k)] = 0$ **then**
        return "no"
return "yes"

We can now see why bloom filters can't suffer from false negatives. When a key k is inserted, the relevant m bits are set to 1. Over the bloom filter's lifetime, bits can change from 0 to 1 but never the reverse. Thus, these m bits remain 1 forevermore. Every subsequent LOOKUP for k is guaranteed to return the correct answer "yes."

We can also see how false positives arise. Suppose that $m = 3$ and the four keys k_1, k_2, k_3, k_4 have the following hash values:

Key	Value of h_1	Value of h_2	Value of h_3
k_1	23	17	5
k_2	5	48	12
k_3	37	8	17
k_4	32	23	2

Suppose we insert k_2, k_3, and k_4 into the bloom filter (Figure 12.6). These three insertions cause a total of nine bits to be set to 1, including the three bits in k_1's footprint (5, 17, and 23). At this point, the bloom filter can no longer distinguish whether or not k_1 has been inserted. Even if k_1 was never inserted into the filter, a LOOKUP for it will return "yes," which is a false positive.

Intuitively, as we make the bloom filter size n bigger, the number of overlaps between the footprints of different keys should decrease, in turn leading to fewer false positives. But the first-order goal of a bloom filter is to save on space. Is there a sweet spot where both n and the frequency of false positives are small simultaneously? The answer is not obvious and requires some mathematical analysis, undertaken in the next section.[30]

---

[30]Spoiler alert: The answer is yes. For example, using 8 bits per key typically leads to a false positive probability of roughly 2% (assuming well-crafted hash functions and a non-pathological data set).

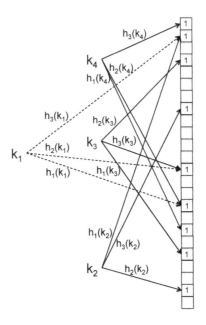

Figure 12.6: False positives: A bloom filter can contain the footprint of a key k_1 even if k_1 was never inserted.

*12.6 Bloom Filters: Heuristic Analysis

The goal of this section is to understand the quantitative trade-off between the space consumption and the frequency of false positives of a bloom filter. That is, how rapidly does the frequency of false positives of a bloom filter decrease as a function of its array length?

If a bloom filter uses a length-n bit array and stores (the footprints of) a set S of keys, the per-key storage in bits is

$$b = \frac{n}{|S|}.$$

We're interested in the case in which b is smaller than the number of bits needed to explicitly store a key or a pointer to an object (which is typically 32 or more). For example, b could be 8 or 16.

12.6.1 Heuristic Assumptions

The relationship between the per-key storage b and the frequency of false positives is not easy to guess, and working it out requires some probability calculations. To understand them, all you need to remember from probability theory is:

The probability that two independent events both occur equals the product of their individual probabilities.

For example, the probability that two independent tosses of a fair 6-sided die are "4" followed by an odd number is $\frac{1}{6} \cdot \frac{3}{6} = \frac{1}{12}$.[31]

To greatly simplify the calculations, we'll make two unjustified assumptions—the same ones we used in passing in our heuristic analyses of hash table performance (Section 12.4.1).

Unjustified Assumptions

1. For every key $k \in U$ in the data set and hash function h_i of the bloom filter, $h_i(k)$ is uniformly distributed, with each of the n array positions equally likely.

2. All of the $h_i(k)$'s, ranging over all keys $k \in U$ and hash functions $h_1, h_2, \ldots, h_m$, are independent random variables.

The first assumption says that, for each key k, each hash function h_i, and each array position $q \in \{0, 1, 2, \ldots, n-1\}$, the probability that $h_i(k) = q$ is exactly $\frac{1}{n}$. The second assumption implies that the probability that $h_i(k_1) = q$ and also $h_j(k_2) = r$ is the product of the individual probabilities, also known as $\frac{1}{n^2}$.

Both assumptions would be legitimate if we randomly chose each of the bloom filter's hash functions independently from the set of all possible hash functions, as in Section 12.3.6. Completely random hash functions are unimplementable (recall Quiz 12.5), so in practice a fixed, "random-like" function is used. This means that in reality, *our heuristic assumptions are false*. With fixed hash functions, every value $h_i(k)$ is completely determined, with no randomness whatsoever. This is why we call the analysis "heuristic."

---

[31]For more background on probability theory, see Appendix B of *Part 1* or the Wikibook on discrete probability (`https://en.wikibooks.org/wiki/High_School_Mathematics_Extensions/Discrete_Probability`).

On Heuristic Analyses

What possible use is a mathematical analysis based on false premises? Ideally, the conclusion of the analysis remains valid in practical situations even though the heuristic assumptions are not satisfied. For bloom filters, the hope is that, provided the data is non-pathological and well-crafted "random-like" hash functions are used, the frequency of false positives behaves *as if* the hash functions were completely random.

You should always be suspicious of a heuristic analysis, and be sure to test its conclusions with a concrete implementation. Happily, empirical studies demonstrate that the frequency of false positives in bloom filters in practice is comparable to the prediction of our heuristic analysis.

12.6.2   The Fraction of Bits Set to 1

We begin with a preliminary calculation.

Quiz 12.7

Suppose a data set S is inserted into a bloom filter that uses m hash functions and a length-n bit array. Under our heuristic assumptions, what is the probability that the array's first bit is set to 1?

a) $\left(\frac{1}{n}\right)^{|S|}$

b) $\left(1 - \frac{1}{n}\right)^{|S|}$

c) $\left(1 - \frac{1}{n}\right)^{m|S|}$

d) $1 - \left(1 - \frac{1}{n}\right)^{m|S|}$

(See Section 12.6.5 for the solution and discussion.)

There is nothing special about the first bit of the bloom filter. By symmetry, the answer to Quiz 12.7 is also the probability that the 7th, or the 23rd, or the 42nd bit is set to 1.

12.6.3   The False Positive Probability

The solution to Quiz 12.7 is messy. To clean it up, we can use the fact that e^x is a good approximation of $1 + x$ when x is close to 0, where $e \approx 2.718\ldots$ is the base of the natural logarithm. This fact is evident from a plot of the two functions:

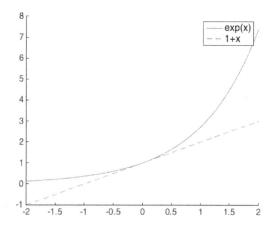

For us, the relevant value of x is $x = -\frac{1}{n}$, which is close to 0 (ignoring the uninteresting case of tiny n). Thus, among friends, we can use the quantity

$$1 - \left(e^{-1/n}\right)^{m|S|} \text{ as a proxy for } 1 - \left(1 - \frac{1}{n}\right)^{m|S|}.$$

We can further simplify the left-hand side to

$$1 - e^{-m|S|/n} = \underbrace{1 - e^{-m/b}}_{\text{estimate of probability that a given bit is 1}},$$

where $b = \frac{n}{|S|}$ denotes the number of bits used per insertion.

Fine, but what about the frequency of false positives? A false positive occurs for a key k not in S when all the m bits $h_1(k), \ldots, h_m(k)$ in its footprint are set to 1 by the keys in S.[32] Because the probability

---

[32] For simplicity, we're assuming that each of the m hash functions hashes k to a different position (as is usually the case).

that a given bit is 1 is approximately $1 - e^{-m/b}$, the probability that all m of these bits are set to 1 is approximately

$$\underbrace{\left(1 - e^{-\frac{m}{b}}\right)^m}_{\text{estimate of false positive frequency}} . \tag{12.2}$$

We can sanity check this estimate by investigating extreme values of b. As the bloom filter grows arbitrarily large (with $b \to \infty$) and is increasingly empty, the estimate (12.2) goes to 0, as we would hope (because e^{-x} goes to 1 as x goes to 0). Conversely, when b is very small, the estimate of the chance of a false positive is large ($\approx 63.2\%$ when $b = m = 1$, for example).[33]

12.6.4   The Punchline

We can use our precise estimate (12.2) of the false positive rate to understand the trade-off between space and accuracy. In addition to the per-key space b, the estimate in (12.2) depends on m, the number of hash functions that the bloom filter uses. The value of m is under complete control of the bloom filter designer, so why not set it to minimize the estimated frequency of errors? That is, holding b fixed, we can choose m to minimize (12.2). Calculus can identify the best choice of m, by setting the derivative of (12.2) with respect to m to 0 and solving for m. You can do the calculations in the privacy of your own home, with the end result being that $(\ln 2) \cdot b \approx 0.693 \cdot b$ is the optimal choice for m. This is not an integer, so round it up or down to get the ideal number of hash functions. For example, when $b = 8$, the number of hash functions m should be either 5 or 6.

We can now specialize the error estimate in (12.2) with the optimal choice of $m = (\ln 2) \cdot b$ to get the estimate

$$\left(1 - e^{-\ln 2}\right)^{(\ln 2)\cdot b} = \left(\frac{1}{2}\right)^{(\ln 2)\cdot b} .$$

---

[33] In addition to our two heuristic assumptions, this analysis cheated twice. First, $e^{-1/n}$ isn't exactly equal to $1 - \frac{1}{n}$, but it's close. Second, even with our heuristic assumptions, the values of two different bits of a bloom filter are not independent—knowing that one bit is 1 makes it slightly more likely that a different bit is 0—but they are close. Both cheats are close approximations of reality (given the heuristic assumptions), and it can be verified both mathematically and empirically that they lead to an accurate conclusion.

This is exactly what we wanted all along—a formula that spits out the expected frequency of false positives as a function of the amount of space we're willing to use.[34] The formula is decreasing *exponentially* with the per-key space b, which is why there is a sweet spot where both the bloom filter size and its frequency of false positives are small simultaneously. For example, with only 8 bits per key stored ($b = 8$), this estimate is slightly over 2%. What if we take $b = 16$ (see Problem 12.3)?

12.6.5   Solution to Quiz 12.7

Correct answer: (d). We can visualize the insertion of the keys in S into the bloom filter as the throwing of darts at a dartboard with n regions, with each dart equally likely to land in each region. Because the bloom filter uses m hash functions, each insertion corresponds to the throwing of m darts, for a total of $m|S|$ darts overall. A dart hitting the ith region corresponds to setting the ith bit of the bloom filter to 1.

By the first heuristic assumption, for every $k \in S$ and $i \in \{1, 2, \ldots, m\}$, the probability that a dart hits the first region (that is, that $h_i(k) = 0$) is $\frac{1}{n}$. Thus, the dart *misses* the first region (that is, $h_i(k)$ is *not* 0) with the remaining probability $1 - \frac{1}{n}$. By the second heuristic assumption, different darts are independent. Thus, the probability that *every* dart misses the first region—that $h_i(k) \neq 0$ for *every* $k \in S$ and $i \in \{1, 2, \ldots, m\}$—is $(1 - \frac{1}{n})^{m|S|}$. With the remaining $1 - (1 - \frac{1}{n})^{m|S|}$ probability, some dart hits the first region (that is, the first bit of the bloom filter is set to 1).

The Upshot

☆ If your application requires fast lookups on an evolving set of objects, the hash table is usually the data structure of choice.

☆ Hash tables support the INSERT and LOOKUP operations, and in some cases the DELETE oper-

---

[34]Equivalently, if you have a target false positive rate of ϵ, you should take the per-key space to be at least $b \approx 1.44 \log_2 \frac{1}{\epsilon}$. As expected, the smaller the target error rate ϵ, the larger the space requirements.

ation. With a well-implemented hash table and non-pathological data, all operations typically run in $O(1)$ time.

☆ A hash table uses a hash function to translate from objects' keys to positions in an array.

☆ Two keys k_1, k_2 collide under a hash function h if $h(k_1) = h(k_2)$. Collisions are inevitable, and a hash table needs a method for resolving them, such as chaining or open addressing.

☆ A good hash function is cheap to evaluate and easy to store, and mimics a random function by spreading non-pathological data sets roughly evenly across the positions of the hash table's array.

☆ Experts have published good hash functions that you can use in your own work.

☆ A hash table should be resized periodically to keep its load small (for example, less than 70%).

☆ For mission-critical code, there's no substitute for trying out multiple competing hash table implementations.

☆ Bloom filters also support the INSERT and LOOKUP operations in constant time, and are preferable to hash tables in applications in which space is at a premium and the occasional false positive is not a dealbreaker.

Test Your Understanding

Problem 12.1 *(S)* Which of the following is *not* a property you would expect a well-designed hash function to have?

a) The hash function should spread out every data set roughly evenly across its range.

b) The hash function should be easy to compute (constant time or close to it).

c) The hash function should be easy to store (constant space or close to it).

d) The hash function should spread out most data sets roughly evenly across its range.

Problem 12.2 *(S)* A good hash function mimics the gold standard of a random function for all practical purposes, so it's interesting to investigate collisions with a random function. If the locations of two different keys $k_1, k_2 \in U$ are chosen independently and uniformly at random across n array positions (with all possibilities equally likely), what is the probability that k_1 and k_2 will collide?

a) 0

b) $\frac{1}{n}$

c) $\frac{2}{n(n-1)}$

d) $\frac{1}{n^2}$

Problem 12.3 We interpreted our heuristic analysis of bloom filters in Section 12.6 by specializing it to the case of 8 bits of space per key inserted into the filter. Suppose we were willing to use twice as much space (16 bits per insertion). What can you say about the corresponding false positive rate, according to our heuristic analysis, assuming that the number m of hash tables is set optimally? (Choose the strongest true statement.)

a) The false positive rate would be less than 1%.

b) The false positive rate would be less than 0.1%.

c) The false positive rate would be less than 0.01%.

d) The false positive rate would be less than 0.001%.

Programming Problems

Problem 12.4 Implement in your favorite programming language the hash table-based solution to the 2-SUM problem in Section 12.2.2. For example, you could generate a list S of one million random integers between -10^{11} and 10^{11}, and count the number of targets t between -10000 and 10000 for which there are distinct $x, y \in S$ with $x + y = t$.

You can use existing implementations of hash tables, or you can implement your own from scratch. In the latter case, compare your performance under different collision-resolution strategies, such as chaining vs. linear probing. (See www.algorithmsilluminated.org for test cases and challenge data sets.)

Appendix C

Quick Review of Asymptotic Notation

This appendix reviews asymptotic notation, especially big-O notation. If you're seeing this material for the first time, you probably want to supplement this appendix with a more thorough treatment, such as Chapter 2 of *Part 1* or the corresponding videos at www.algorithmsilluminated.org. If you have seen it before, don't feel compelled to read this appendix from front to back—dip in as needed wherever you need a refresher.

C.1 The Gist

Asymptotic notation identifies a sweet spot of granularity for reasoning about algorithms and data structures. It is coarse enough to suppress all the details you want to ignore—details that depend on the choice of architecture, the choice of programming language, the choice of compiler, and so on. On the other hand, it's precise enough to make useful comparisons between different high-level algorithmic approaches to solving a problem, especially on larger inputs (the inputs that require algorithmic ingenuity).

A good seven-word summary of asymptotic notation is:

> **Asymptotic Notation in Seven Words**
>
> suppress $\underbrace{constant\ factors}_{too\ system\text{-}dependent}$ and $\underbrace{lower\text{-}order\ terms}_{irrelevant\ for\ large\ inputs}$

The most important concept in asymptotic notation is big-O notation. Intuitively, saying that something is $O(f(n))$ for a function $f(n)$ means that $f(n)$ is what you're left with after suppressing constant factors and lower-order terms. For example, if $g(n) = 6n\log_2 n + 6n$, then $g(n) = O(n \log n)$.[1] Big-O notation buckets algorithms and data structure operations into groups according to their asymptotic worst-case running times, such as linear-time ($O(n)$) or logarithmic-time ($O(\log n)$) algorithms and operations.

C.2   Big-O Notation

Big-O notation concerns functions $T(n)$ defined on the positive integers $n = 1, 2, \ldots$. For us, $T(n)$ will almost always denote a bound on the worst-case running time of an algorithm or data structure operation, as a function of the size n of the input.

Big-O Notation (English Version)

$T(n) = O(f(n))$ if and only if $T(n)$ is eventually bounded above by a constant multiple of $f(n)$.

Here is the corresponding mathematical definition of big-O notation, the definition you should use in formal proofs.

Big-O Notation (Mathematical Version)

$T(n) = O(f(n))$ if and only if there exist positive constants c and n_0 such that

$$T(n) \leq c \cdot f(n) \tag{C.1}$$

for all $n \geq n_0$.

The constant c quantifies the "constant multiple" and the constant n_0 quantifies "eventually." For example, in Figure C.1, the constant c corresponds to 3, while n_0 corresponds to the crossover point between the functions $T(n)$ and $c \cdot f(n)$.

A Word of Caution

When we say that c and n_0 are constants, we mean they *cannot depend on* n. For example, in

---

[1]When ignoring constant factors, we don't need to specify the base of the logarithm. (Different logarithmic functions differ only by a constant factor.)

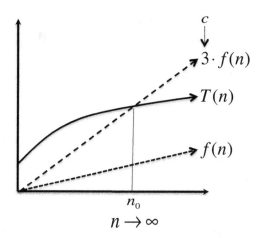

Figure C.1: A picture illustrating when $T(n) = O(f(n))$. The constant c quantifies the "constant multiple" of $f(n)$, and the constant n_0 quantifies "eventually."

Figure C.1, c and n_0 were fixed numbers (like 3 or 1000), and we then considered the inequality (C.1) as n grows arbitrarily large (looking rightward on the graph toward infinity). If you ever find yourself saying "take $n_0 = n$" or "take $c = \log_2 n$" in an alleged big-O proof, you need to start over with choices of c and n_0 that are independent of n.

C.3   Examples

We claim that if $T(n)$ is a polynomial with some degree k, then $T(n) = O(n^k)$. Thus, big-O notation really is suppressing constant factors and lower-order terms.

Proposition C.1 *Suppose*

$$T(n) = a_k n^k + \cdots a_1 n + a_0,$$

where $k \geq 0$ is a nonnegative integer and the a_i's are real numbers (positive or negative). Then $T(n) = O(n^k)$.

Proof: Proving a big-O statement boils down to reverse engineering appropriate values for the constants c and n_0. Here, to keep things easy to follow, we'll pull values for these constants out of a hat: $n_0 = 1$ and c equal to the sum of absolute values of the coefficients:[2]

$$c = |a_k| + \cdots + |a_1| + |a_0|.$$

Both these numbers are independent of n. We now must show that these choices of constants satisfy the definition, meaning that $T(n) \leq c \cdot n^k$ for all $n \geq n_0 = 1$.

To verify this inequality, fix a positive integer $n \geq n_0 = 1$. We need a sequence of upper bounds on $T(n)$, culminating in an upper bound of $c \cdot n^k$. First let's apply the definition of $T(n)$:

$$T(n) = a_k n^k + \cdots + a_1 n + a_0.$$

If we take the absolute value of each coefficient a_i on the right-hand side, the expression only becomes larger. ($|a_i|$ can only be bigger than a_i, and because n^i is positive, $|a_i| n^i$ can only be bigger than $a_i n^i$.) This means that

$$T(n) \leq |a_k| n^k + \cdots + |a_1| n + |a_0|.$$

Now that the coefficients are nonnegative, we can use a similar trick to turn the different powers of n into a common power of n. As $n \geq 1$, n^k is only bigger than n^i for every $i \in \{0, 1, 2, \ldots, k\}$. Because $|a_i|$ is nonnegative, $|a_i| n^k$ is only bigger than $|a_i| n^i$. This means that

$$T(n) \leq |a_k| n^k + \cdots + |a_1| n^k + |a_0| n^k = \underbrace{(|a_k| + \cdots + |a_1| + |a_0|)}_{=c} \cdot n^k.$$

This inequality holds for every $n \geq n_0 = 1$, which is exactly what we wanted to prove. $\mathscr{QED}$

We can also use the definition of big-O notation to argue that one function is *not* big-O of another function.

Proposition C.2 *If $T(n) = 2^{10n}$, then $T(n)$ is not $O(2^n)$.*

---

[2]Recall that the *absolute value* $|x|$ of a real number x equals x when $x \geq 0$, and $-x$ when $x \leq 0$. In particular, $|x|$ is always nonnegative.

Proof: The usual way to prove that one function is not big-O of another is by contradiction. So, assume the opposite of the statement in the proposition, that $T(n)$ is, in fact, $O(2^n)$. By the definition of big-O notation, there are positive constants c and n_0 such that

$$2^{10n} \leq c \cdot 2^n$$

for all $n \geq n_0$. As 2^n is a positive number, we can cancel it from both sides of this inequality to derive

$$2^{9n} \leq c$$

for all $n \geq n_0$. But this inequality is patently false: The right-hand side is a fixed constant (independent of n), while the left-hand side goes to infinity as n grows large. This shows that our assumption that $T(n) = O(2^n)$ cannot be correct, and we can conclude that 2^{10n} is not $O(2^n)$. $\mathcal{QED}$

C.4   Big-Omega and Big-Theta Notation

Big-O notation is by far the most important and ubiquitous concept for discussing the asymptotic running times of algorithms and data structure operations. A couple of its close relatives, the big-omega and big-theta notations, are also worth knowing. If big-O is analogous to "less than or equal to ($\leq$)," then big-omega and big-theta are analogous to "greater than or equal to ($\geq$)," and "equal to ($=$)," respectively.

The formal definition of big-omega notation parallels that of big-O notation. In English, we say that one function $T(n)$ is big-omega of another function $f(n)$ if and only if $T(n)$ is eventually bounded *below* by a constant multiple of $f(n)$. In this case, we write $T(n) = \Omega(f(n))$. As before, we use two constants c and n_0 to quantify "constant multiple" and "eventually."

Big-Omega Notation

$T(n) = \Omega(f(n))$ if and only if there exist positive constants c and n_0 such that
$$T(n) \geq c \cdot f(n)$$
for all $n \geq n_0$.

Big-theta notation, or simply theta notation, is analogous to "equal to." Saying that $T(n) = \Theta(f(n))$ simply means that both $T(n) = \Omega(f(n))$ and $T(n) = O(f(n))$. Equivalently, $T(n)$ is eventually sandwiched between two different constant multiples of $f(n)$.

Big-Theta Notation

$T(n) = \Theta(f(n))$ if and only if there exist positive constants c_1, c_2, and n_0 such that

$$c_1 \cdot f(n) \leq T(n) \leq c_2 \cdot f(n)$$

for all $n \geq n_0$.

A Word of Caution

Because algorithm designers are so focused on running time guarantees (which are upper bounds), they tend to use big-O notation even when big-theta notation would be more accurate; for example, stating the running time of an algorithm as $O(n)$ even when it's clearly $\Theta(n)$.

The next quiz checks your understanding of big-O, big-omega, and big-theta notation.

Quiz C.1

Let $T(n) = \frac{1}{2}n^2 + 3n$. Which of the following statements are true? (Choose all that apply.)

a) $T(n) = O(n)$

b) $T(n) = \Omega(n)$

c) $T(n) = \Theta(n^2)$

d) $T(n) = O(n^3)$

> (See below for the solution and discussion.)

Correct answers: (b),(c),(d). The final three responses are all correct, and hopefully the intuition for why is clear. $T(n)$ is a quadratic function. The linear term $3n$ doesn't matter for large n, so we should expect that $T(n) = \Theta(n^2)$ (answer (c)). This automatically implies that $T(n) = \Omega(n^2)$ and hence $T(n) = \Omega(n)$ also (answer (b)). Similarly, $T(n) = \Theta(n^2)$ implies that $T(n) = O(n^2)$ and hence also $T(n) = O(n^3)$ (answer (d)). Proving these statements formally boils down to exhibiting appropriate constants to satisfy the definitions. For example, taking $n_0 = 1$ and $c = \frac{1}{2}$ proves (b). Taking $n_0 = 1$ and $c = 4$ proves (d). Combining these constants ($n_0 = 1$, $c_1 = \frac{1}{2}$, $c_2 = 4$) proves (c). A proof by contradiction, in the spirit of Proposition C.2, shows that (a) is not a correct answer.

Solutions to Selected Problems

Problem 7.1: Conditions (a) and (c) are satisfied by some sparse graphs (such as a star graph) and some dense graphs (such as a complete graph with one extra edge glued on). Condition (b) is satisfied only by sparse graphs, and condition (d) only by dense graphs.

Problem 7.2: (c). Scan through the row corresponding to v in the adjacency matrix.

Problem 8.1: All four statements hold: (a) by the UCC algorithm in Section 8.3; (b) by the Augmented-BFS algorithm in Section 8.2; (c) by the Kosaraju algorithm in Section 8.6; and (d) by the TopoSort algorithm in Section 8.5.

Problem 8.2: (c). $\Omega(n^2)$ time is required because, in the worst case, a correct algorithm must look at each of the n^2 entries of the adjacency matrix at least once. $O(n^2)$ time is achievable, for example by constructing the adjacency list representation of the input graph with a single pass over the adjacency matrix (in $O(n^2)$ time) and then running DFS with the new representation in $O(m + n) = O(n^2)$ time.

Problem 8.7: (c). Computing the "magical ordering" in the first pass of the Kosaraju algorithm requires depth-first search. (See the proof of Theorem 8.10.) In the second pass, given the magical ordering of the vertices, any instantiation of the GenericSearch algorithm (including BFS) will successfully discover the SCCs in reverse topological order.

Problem 8.8: (a),(b). The modification in (a) does not change the order in which the algorithm considers vertices in its second pass, and so it remains correct. The modification in (b) is equivalent to running the Kosaraju algorithm on the reversal of the input graph. Because a graph and its reversal have exactly the same SCCs (Quiz 8.6), the algorithm remains correct. The modifications in (c) and (d) are equivalent, as in the argument for (a) above, and do not result in a correct algorithm. For a counterexample, revisit our running example (and especially the discussion on page 59).

Problem 9.2: (b). Two sums of distinct powers of 2 cannot be the same. (Imagine the numbers are written in binary.) For (a) and (c), there are counterexamples with three vertices and three edges.

Problem 9.3: (c),(d). Statement (d) holds because, when P has only one edge, every path goes up in length by at least as much as P does. This also shows that (b) is false. An example similar to the one in Section 9.3.1 shows that (a) is false, and it follows that (c) is true.

Problem 9.7: In lines 4 and 6 of the `Dijkstra` algorithm (page 80), respectively, replace $len(v)+\ell_{vw}$ with $\max\{len(v), \ell_{vw}\}$ and $len(v^*)+\ell_{v^*w^*}$ with $\max\{len(v^*), \ell_{v^*w^*}\}$.

Problem 10.1: (b),(c). The raison d'être of a heap is to support fast minimum computations, with `HeapSort` (Section 10.3.1) being a canonical application. Negating the key of every object turns a heap into a data structure that supports fast maximum computations. Heaps do not generally support fast lookups unless you happen to be looking for the object with the minimum key.

Problem 10.4: (a). Only the object with the smallest key can be extracted with one heap operation. Calling EXTRACTMIN five successive times returns the object in the heap with the fifth-smallest key. Extracting the object with the median or maximum key would require a linear number of heap operations.

Problem 10.5: In line 14 of the heap-based implementation of `Dijkstra` (page 111), replace $len(w^*)+\ell_{w^*y}$ with $\max\{len(w^*), \ell_{w^*y}\}$.

Problem 11.1: (a). Statement (a) holds because there are at most 2^i nodes in the ith level of a binary tree, and hence at most $1 + 2 + 4 + \cdots + 2^i \leq 2^{i+1}$ nodes in levels 0 through i combined. Accommodating n nodes requires $2^{h+1} \geq n$, where h is the tree height, so $h = \Omega(\log n)$. Statement (b) holds for balanced binary search trees but is generally false for unbalanced binary search trees (see footnote 4 in Chapter 11).

Statement (c) is false because the heap and search tree properties are incomparable (see page 132). Statement (d) is false, as a sorted array is preferable to a balanced binary search tree when the set of objects to be stored is static, with no insertions or deletions (see page 131).

Problem 12.1: (a). Pathological data sets show that property (a) is impossible and so cannot be expected (see Section 12.3.6). The other three properties are satisfied by state-of-the-art hash functions.

Problem 12.2: (b). There are n possibilities for k_1's location and n possibilities for k_2's location, for a total of n^2 outcomes. Of these, k_1 and k_2 collide in exactly n of them—the outcome in which both are assigned the first position, the outcome in which both are assigned the second position, and so on. Because every outcome is equally likely (with probability $\frac{1}{n^2}$ each), the probability of a collision is $n \cdot \frac{1}{n^2} = \frac{1}{n}$.

Index

CPSIA information can be obtained
at www.ICGtesting.com
Printed in the USA
LVHW041123141222
735149LV00002B/199